FEARLESS RELATIONSHIPS

FEARLESS RELATIONSHIPS

Simple Rules for Lifelong Contentment

By Karen Casey

Hazelden
Center City, Minnesota 55012-0176

1-800-328-0094
1-651-213-4590 (Fax)
www.hazelden.org

Library of Congress Cataloging-in-Publication Data

Casey, Karen.
   Fearless relationships : simple rules for lifelong contentment /
by Karen Casey.
      p. cm.
   ISBN 1-56838-985-X (paperback)
   1. Interpersonal relations. I. Title.
   HM1106.C375 2003
   158.2—dc21

                                              2002038886

07 06 05 04 03   6 5 4 3 2 1

Cover design by David Spohn
Interior design by Rachel Holscher
Typesetting by Stanton Publication Services, Inc.

☙ Contents

∾ Introduction

Exploring what helps and what hinders relationships has intrigued me for years. I have had many relationships, of course, in my sixty-three years. Sometimes my behavior improved relationships, and sometimes, unfortunately, my behavior hindered relationships.

For the first thirty-six years of my life, I did not understand which of my actions hindered and which helped my relationships. Since getting into recovery from addiction more than twenty-seven years ago, I have developed a keen interest in observing my own and others' behavior. The dynamics that foretell of a successful relationship have interested me the most. Those dynamics are the rules that I share with you in the chapters that follow.

Experience has taught me that the simple rules discussed in this book really can form the basis of a healthy relationship. Each short chapter is devoted to one simple rule. The order of the rules is arbitrary. All are equally important; one or all of them, when applied, will peacefully enhance every relationship in our lives. Each chapter ends with some final thoughts that I call Touch Points. These Touch Points are intended to serve as concise reminders of how uncomplicated it is to work toward peaceful interpersonal relationships.

I believe that healing relationships is our common goal as members of society. As this world begins to seem more treacherous since the tragedy of September 11, 2001, there is no better time to seek to make our relationships, all of them, more peaceful.

We will not heal individually or as a society, and certainly not as a multicultural world, unless we heal our many personal relationships. And there is no better day than this one to begin the process.

The willingness to improve relations with others, including loved ones, colleagues, and even strangers, is the first important step to creating a world that will nurture us all.

Seek to Understand Every Situation from a Fresh Perspective

Choosing this particular rule as the first rule of a peaceful relationship wasn't entirely by chance. If you and I practiced this one rule in any experience that triggered even slight agitation in us, we would save ourselves from countless arguments, some minor, many major.

What does it mean to *seek to understand every situation from a fresh perspective?* It's quite simple, really. In any encounter with another person, there are two perspectives or viewpoints being expressed: yours and the other person's. These differing viewpoints aren't necessarily problematic in every instance. Two people may simply be having a conversation to pass the time and they feel no need for agreement. But when the conversation is about a situation that needs a resolution or reflects opposing opinions on a topic that is near and dear to both parties, tension often arises, and acknowledging the dissimilar perspectives becomes necessary.

It's at this point that seeking to understand, or allowing for, a different perspective or perception is beneficial. This does not mean you have to embrace the other perspective as your own, but letting your adversary continue to have his or her opinion without allowing it to destroy your day or your relationship is both respectful and healthy.

Being able to live comfortably in a world which expresses thousands of heartfelt perspectives is becoming far more important with the passage of time and the clashing of cultures.

Because of our instant access to news around the world, we are bombarded by constant information and can hear contrasting perspectives on events that happen all over the globe. What we take away from this inundation of information is naturally what feeds the viewpoints we then so dearly cling to, and don't easily relinquish.

Deciding to switch perspectives, to exchange ours for one an adversary holds, does not mean we are weak or uncommitted to a particular set of values or philosophy. It may mean we allowed ourselves to be re-educated. Or perhaps we decided that the idea we were hanging on to didn't deserve our adherence any longer. For some of us, giving in to another perspective might mean that we made a choice to be peaceful rather than tense.

I can remember as though it were yesterday the first time I consciously chose to walk away from an argument rather than fight for an opinion that I knew really didn't matter in the larger picture of my life. Until that time, I had not actually appreciated that I could make this choice. I had been fighting with other adults my entire life. As the third child in a family of four kids, I had fought everyone's battles, including my mom's, against my domineering, angry dad far into adulthood. This pattern of behavior was constant.

As adults, we generally carry into all other relationships those behaviors we mastered in our families of origin. My argumentative nature went with me into my first marriage. My husband and I didn't quarrel constantly, but we disagreed often and I became a master at using silence or passive aggression, coupled with long-held resentment, to make my point when words couldn't. Either way, the outcome was the same: no resolution and certainly no peace. For twelve years our lives were tension filled and our minds, on myriad issues, remained unchanged. Our relationship brought little comfort to either of us. Naturally, it ended. Neither of us was willing or able to shift our perspective on the meaningful issues in our lives, nor were we ever willing to choose peace over the insistence that we were right.

And then, in 1975, my life dramatically changed. Through a series of significant, and not coincidental, interactions with friends and colleagues, I ended up at a Twelve Step recovery meeting, and my worldview began to change. I had never planned on changing my life or my outlook in such specific ways, but the ideas being exchanged in this circle of people immediately captured my imagination.

At my first Twelve Step meeting, in the basement of the Unitarian church in southeast Minneapolis, I was introduced to the idea that I didn't have to react, in any way, to the behaviors or the opinions of others. I had never considered *not reacting* as a viable alternative to reacting. Throughout my entire life, I had been intent on being heard, being understood, and being right!

Yet there I sat, listening to a group of happy men and women sharing their experiences, strengths, and hopes, and it was evident that they were making clear choices based on their specific needs. The results of their choices were thoughtful actions, never the hasty, angry reactions that were so typical of my behavior.

I knew the wisdom of what they were saying, and I knew I was familiar with the underlying idea, but I just couldn't recall where I had heard it before. I left my first meeting eager to know more about the set of beliefs that seemed to make these men and women so happy. I was truly astounded to realize that there was another way to live and that it was possible to let others have whatever idea or perspective made them happy. Furthermore, I could still keep my own perspectives if they continued to bring me happiness.

Following this first rule, seek to understand every situation from a fresh perspective, will eliminate most of the disagreements that surface in our lives. Our disagreements are often rooted in past hurts. Deciding to let go of past hurts is what this rule is all about.

Touch Points

1. When in conversation today, quiet your own mind, completely. This response will not come naturally.
2. Next, focus intently on every word the other person is saying. When your mind wanders, bring it back.
3. Then listen with your heart.
4. In your heart, change places with the other speaker. Be him or her for a moment. How does it feel?
5. Ask yourself, is my perspective more important than my peace of mind?

6. Seek the willingness to let go of your own perspective. Ask your Higher Power for help.
7. Take note that your perspective is related to your past, never the present moment.
8. Feel the change in mood as you let your own perspective go.
9. Feel the tension leave your body.
10. Note the change in your companion's body language too.
11. Be grateful for the willingness to be at peace.

2

Be Kind No Matter What

I was first introduced to the idea of being kind no matter what in the early '70s through a book by John Powell. I had chosen *Why Am I Afraid To Tell You Who I Am?* as a text for a journal writing class I was teaching while in graduate school. In the early pages of the book, Powell recounts an episode that occurred while he and a friend strolled down a New York City street.

They had stopped to buy a newspaper and the street corner vendor was extremely rude to Powell's friend. Powell noted that this same vendor treated his friend this way every morning. His friend was always very kind to the vendor and tipped him every morning. Powell asked him why he continued to be so nice when the vendor was clearly deserving of a rebuff rather than kindness. His friend said, "Why should I let him decide what kind of a day I am going to have?"

When I read this simple passage I felt like I had hit the jackpot! At that moment I realized my entire life had been about letting others decide what kind of day or hour or moment I was going to have. Taking complete charge of my actions or feelings was a totally foreign idea. I had quite willingly been held hostage my entire life by other people's behavior. What an eye-opener Powell's story was!

Choosing to be kind in ordinary encounters is not difficult, but in certain encounters, kindness may not be prudent, especially if you are female, alone, and unfamiliar with your surroundings. However, you can generally choose to walk away rather than become engaged verbally. Just remember, being unkind is never the best response.

In ordinary experiences, if a kind response isn't forthcoming, the next step is to walk away without becoming engaged, especially if the encounter has turned unpleasant. This takes willingness, effort, and the commitment to take charge of your every thought, but the payoff is transforming. I know. I have experienced it!

Indeed, I re-experience this transformation daily. Is this because I have a tendency to surround myself with unpleasant people? I think not. It's because I, like you, live *in the world of people* and most of them would like to be in charge, not only of their own life, but of mine and yours too. That's the way life is in our human community.

Dozens of times a day, we have the opportunity to practice this rule of kindness. Making the choice to be kind to whomever we share breakfast with is a good place to begin. It doesn't mean we have to talk at length, or at all, if we feel the need for silence. It simply means we can share how we feel with a smile and then be quiet.

Being kind takes so little effort. It's often nothing more than an expression we might wear on our face, or a nod in someone's direction. It's maintaining eye contact when speaking with another person. It's standing or sitting still while another person is directing a comment or a question to us. It's acknowledging the people around us in the grocery store or the restaurant. It's being *present* when someone is attempting to get our attention.

Some years ago I heard a wonderful story about the Dali Lama. He was invited to give an address to a prestigious California crowd following a fund-raising dinner. He walked slowly to the podium after being introduced. He very quietly surveyed the crowd for a few moments and then said, "Your assignment in this life is to love one another." After speaking those few words, he walked back to his seat.

The crowd seemed quite dissatisfied that his address was so short. After all, they had paid for far more. But then he rose again, and headed back to the podium. His movement was met with sighs of relief and approval. Once again, he stood very quietly before his audience and said ever so gently into the microphone, "And if you can't love one another, at least don't hurt one another." He then walked off the stage.

His words are timeless wisdom, the only wisdom any of us needs if we have the desire to live in our communities peacefully. Have you refrained from hurting anyone today?

TOUCH POINTS

1. Upon arising every morning, ask your Higher Power to help you be kind.
2. Pause a moment before answering a question. In that moment, remember kindness.

3. Remember that being kind doesn't mean you have to agree with the other person.
4. Being kind means using a soft voice.
5. Being kind means not using hurtful words.
6. Being kind means speaking from the heart.
7. Kindness can be practiced until it becomes real.
8. Acting as if we feel kind is just as good as feeling kind to begin with.
9. Kindness is a habit.
10. Kindness isn't weakness.
11. Kindness can transform a hateful situation and a hateful person, ourselves included.
12. Only one person has to be kind for a situation to dramatically change.
13. Being kind changes us beyond our wildest expectations.

3

Listen, Then Comment If Necessary

Listening fully to what another person is saying to us shouldn't need to be a rule, but my own experience has proven otherwise. Do you ever plan your response to what someone is saying before they have even finished speaking? It's a behavior I have fought against for years. And I am thrilled to be able to say that I have made progress! It has come about only because of my persistence. Being willing to actually listen, completely, to another person's entire thought is not an easy task.

I don't think it's unusual to constantly entertain drivel or even serious opinions in our minds while in the midst of conversations with others. Wanting to control all situations, and thus the people in our lives, means wanting to have the last word in any discussion. The only way to accomplish this, we think, is to be ready with an answer or a solution for every point in a conversation as soon as the other person has quit speaking. Many times even before, to tell the truth.

Having our response in mind ahead of time becomes the way we try to manage the outcomes in our lives. Our folly is that because our focus was not on listening to the other person in the first place, we seldom offer the right response.

Perhaps not being listened to as children has contributed to our need to win every argument, or at least to have the final say. It doesn't matter why we behave this way, but every time we do, we are harming the other person as well as ourselves. It is not coincidental that we have been drawn into the company of certain people. They have wisdom or information we need. Any time we interrupt the message they are offering with an idea of our own, one either spoken or simply coddled in our mind, we are missing a thought we need to experience.

Looking at our relations with all people from this perspective can dramatically change how we interpret each one of them. And it does make it easier to listen more completely every time we are in the company of another person. With practice, it can become exciting to speculate about where each new piece of information might be leading us. We can be certain that every bit of information has its part to play in our development.

If you doubt this, spend a few moments reflecting on some of your past experiences. My first marriage often comes to mind when I consider how I came to be here, doing what I am doing with my life. The pain of the past seems like a very small price to have paid. And without those specific experiences, I would not have so willingly sought the help I found in recovery. The rest is history.

Making a living as a writer, having a Ph.D. from the University of Minnesota, living in Florida during the winter months with my wonderful second husband, and riding my own Harley all over the country are outcomes I would never have imagined for my life.

Marrying my first husband while at Purdue, developing a dependency on alcohol, other drugs, and men, and then moving to Minnesota, opened the door to the journey that has carried me to this very spot, a journey that was mine to make. And I couldn't be happier! I have come to believe that God's plan for us is far grander than our own plan.

Learning to listen to the messages that were meant for my spiritual development didn't happen without resistance. This is no doubt true for each of us. Unless we are familiar with the idea that *we will be told what we need to know when the time is right*, we will no doubt miss the message. But it will come again. It will come as often as necessary until we finally surrender to it.

One of the most reassuring things I have learned on this spiritual path is that I will not be able to avoid learning what I need to learn. The lessons will come again and again until I acknowledge them and let them infiltrate my life.

We can save hours, days, maybe months of frustration by deciding to listen now, while the messages are fresh. Listening will be helpful to the people sharing our path as well. Remember, they are not on our path coincidentally. The messages they share with us are part of their evolution too.

I have learned in twenty-seven years of recovery that many of the ideas others share need no response at all. Often people are simply venting their feelings and don't want a response. I didn't know this for the first thirty-six years of my life. I thought I needed to respond to everything people said to me, and that it better be the right response or I'd look like a fool.

Many relationships are endangered by the need we feel to make a response when one isn't actually necessary. But until we experience the freedom of making no response, we can't appreciate the *holiness* of this idea. And unless we are in perpetual solitary confinement, we will be in relationship with others. From my perspective, that's by design.

Our work in this life is to have and to heal relationships. Learning what this means can take a lifetime. Accomplishing it takes a willingness most will have to cultivate.

A very simple beginning is to practice the statement: *I need say nothing.* In fact, even when a response is required, it need not be made instantly. Seeking clarity about the right response is possible only in the quiet spaces of your mind. Listen. Listen to the other person. Listen to yourself. Only then, respond. And never forget: *the right response may be no response at all.*

Touch Points

1. Listening is first and foremost a decision.
2. The freedom to say nothing is empowering.
3. Listening becomes easier with practice.
4. Listening intently will clarify the response that is necessary.
5. Listening fosters peace of mind.
6. Listening is a tool for healing relationships.
7. Through listening, we will receive the messages we are ready for.
8. Listening is honoring another.
9. Listening is honoring God.
10. Listening is honoring the world community.
11. Our response after careful listening is our gift to the moment which eventually touches us all.

4

Pray for Understanding of Others

Does praying for the understanding of others seem too simple to be considered a rule for better relationships? It is certainly not an original idea. I almost discarded it when it first came to mind, but after thoughtful reflection I decided to keep it as a rule. Let me tell you why.

The prayer part of this rule is what makes it so important. Think for a moment what the act of prayer is and what it does for you while I recount for you what I think it is and what it does for me.

Prayer quiets my mind. It lessens the hold my ego has over my thoughts, at least for the moment. When I pray, I imagine a vision of God as I understand God, resting, yet at attention. I further imagine myself holding out my hands as they cradle the problem that has caused my fear. I can pray in this manner with my eyes wide open, even while still present in the situation that triggered my need to pray. No one has to know that I am praying.

I then imagine God taking the problem from me and blowing it away. Almost immediately I feel feather light with no problem holding me down. When I return my mind to the present circumstances, whatever they are, they appear different. If a person has caused my anxiety, he or she appears soft and vulnerable now. No longer am I fearful, and the solution to the dilemma signals to me.

Prayer is a form of surrender, of giving up, of quieting down. It allows us to hear the inner messenger who understands our need. Being attentive to the messenger and then being willing to carry the message sent assures us that we can do or say the next right thing. The relationship will benefit.

This brings to mind a time when practicing this method resulted in a significantly awesome turn of events in my life. I was in a meeting with a professor who was a member of my Ph.D. dissertation committee at the University of Minnesota. He had missed three deadlines for reading my dissertation. The rest of the committee had sent me their comments and had given me passing marks. I was desperate for him to finish his work because my oral exam was already scheduled.

I began to dread this professor's response to my work because his body language was extremely negative. Suddenly he said, "This entire dissertation has to be rewritten." I was stunned and felt sick. There were only three weeks until the oral and my major professor was leaving on a year's sabbatical right after that date. I did not have enough time to rewrite a three hundred page dissertation.

At first I could find no words to reply at all. Then I quietly asked him to share his criticisms, all the while asking my Higher Power to help me remain calm while responding to them. I suggested that we go through each section, allowing me a chance to answer each criticism. Much to my surprise, he agreed. What happened next has no rational explanation.

God offered me an explanation for every criticism the

professor had just moments before I needed to give it. I felt like I was outside of my body, looking on. The professor asked his questions, and it was as if I *heard* him being answered by *my own voice*, not as if I actually answered him.

For more than three hours we sat in his office discussing point after point. Following each of my answers, he quietly said, "Yes, I see." When we finally reached the conclusion, he smiled at me, for the first time, and said that it was a great piece of work. He stood, shook my hand, and said he was satisfied and that I deserved the degree. I left his office with his signature in hand. I could not remember how I had responded to any question or criticism. I was sure of only one thing: God spoke, and my professor heard the words.

Tears flooded my eyes as I raced to my car. I had prayed for help and understanding and they came! I moved out of the way, allowing God to step in. The professor softened while I shared "the message." The resolution brought peace to both of us.

I had been told ever since entering Twelve Step recovery that God worked in this way, but I had never tested the process. I cherish this experience, and it has served me well on many occasions, as a sponsor and in my own recovery.

Your Higher Power doesn't always respond in such a dramatic way, at least not in my experience, but the solution to every single problem within every single relationship is never more than a prayer away. We simply have to want the solution and be willing to do the footwork. We have to be willing to believe that any situation is not an accident but an opportunity for us to grow.

It's safe to say that every problem you and I will have in

our lifetime will involve a relationship, even if it's not a primary one. For instance, dealing with an angry neighbor over a missing newspaper or a condescending salesperson at your favorite department store might be the cause of inner turmoil. However, no matter who is on the other end of our turmoil, the solution is the same. Prayer. Pray for understanding of that person. Pray for his or her peace, and your own. Pray for the willingness to forgive and move on. Finally, be grateful for the opportunity to turn once again to God for help. Every time we do so, we make a contribution that is helping to heal the world.

Touch Points

1. Prayer quiets our minds.
2. Prayer refreshes us.
3. Prayer makes it possible for us to *see* the solution to our problem.
4. Prayer changes every outcome.
5. Prayer changes us.
6. Praying gives us something to do when we feel lost and afraid.
7. Prayer changes how we see everyone on our path.
8. Prayer seems to change everyone in our life, but it's we who change. The result is the same.
9. Prayer has an infinite power.
10. Prayer will change the course of our history.

∽ 5
Every Person We Meet Is a Learning Partner

This rule may seem formidable at first glance. Viewing every person as a learning partner implies that we are constantly *working*. Yet when viewed from another perspective, it could make our lives feel more exciting and purposeful. The so-called "chance" meetings we find so interesting or unusual or unexpected are not by chance at all.

When I first heard this idea, I was filled with both dread and anticipation. The dread was because I thought it meant I could never really relax and just be me. I thought it meant I had to be fully prepared to respond in just the right way every time someone spoke to me or even glanced in my direction. I feared that I might blow some major chance that would affect my entire future if I didn't impress a particular person in the correct manner.

My positive anticipation, on the other hand, was due to the possibility that this journey was quite unique and couldn't be made by anyone else in exactly the same way I was making it. I loved this possibility. I loved being necessary to the grand scheme of the universe. I loved thinking that every one of my experiences had a reason for happening.

Believing that every person who shares even a single

moment of our life is a learning partner, can make our lives feel so much more meaningful, so much more intentional. I have chosen to interpret this rule this way, and it has taught me to feel relief rather than confusion, joy rather than distress, acceptance rather than anger, forgiveness rather than resentment.

Believing that every person in our lives is put there by design can make each new introduction seem like an adventure. Consider for a moment the most recent person you met. No matter what your feelings or thoughts are about that person, you can decide to trust that he or she is part of your destiny. Something you are destined to eventually learn may surface through the interaction that transpires between you. Either way, it's not an accident that certain people show up in our lives. With practice we can learn to rejoice over each and every experience. The lessons we learn through others are *divine*.

I have come to cherish this rule because it makes all of my past experiences valuable and understandable. It's not uncommon to second guess our earlier decisions. We may regret personal stands we took with family or friends, but we can instead celebrate these as points on our learning curve. We are students, after all, and relationships are our teachers.

I used to journal, endlessly, about the many crises in my life. I was always in turmoil. My fears were rampant. I never measured up, or so I thought. I was constantly certain I was about to be rejected or had just been rejected and was *crying in my beer*, oftentimes, literally. I had no real outlet for my many disappointments and perpetual anxiety, so I filled notebook after notebook with my pitiful thoughts. Poor me! My journals covered the same kinds of situations over and over.

It was not until I found Twelve Step recovery that I was able to see how my many bad decisions and unhealthy relationships had played necessary roles in the drama that was my life. If it had not been for these many detours along the way, I would not be here now, doing what I so love doing.

I married, the first time, a man who was as insecure as I was—an alcoholic. I had no idea that alcohol was the root of his problem, nor did I ever imagine that drinking would become the explanation for my problems too. I married him simply because he asked me to and I didn't think anyone else would. I was sure I could change him. I had no idea that I was on *this path* to join him.

I mention my first husband to illustrate the importance of every relationship we have and because people often ask if I am sorry I married him. They ask if I think I could have prevented my own alcoholism if I had not married an alcoholic. The answer to both questions is no.

My first husband was a learning partner I needed to fulfill a role I was destined to play. And each other person, before and after him, has played his or her part in my drama as well. The same can be said for you.

Touch Points

1. Never disregard anyone you meet. Each person is part of your destiny.
2. Every conversation is meaningful. Listen closely.

3. Our journey is a series of learning partnerships.
4. Be glad for each lesson, each day.
5. Difficult relationships offer key lessons.
6. All relationships were hand-picked by us for the lessons we need to master.
7. Don't shy away from any person. His or her presence is by design.
8. Any lesson can be refused for the time being. It will come again.
9. Our learning partners need us as much as we need them.
10. The people who seem to appear again and again are being drawn to us. Be grateful.
11. We don't have to love our learning partners. We simply have to acknowledge them and stay open to the lesson being presented.
12. The learning partners we need will follow us.
13. Surrender to the lessons.

☞ 6

Our Lessons Will Be Repeated Until We Learn Them

This rule is very comforting. It allows me to relax and not fret so much about missing opportunities for growth when they are first presented. Just knowing that every lesson I need to learn will make its way to me, as many times as is necessary, lets me take charge of when I learn these lessons.

Looking at life's experiences from this perspective, *as a body of lessons or opportunities*, isn't a commonly held idea, unfortunately. I know many people, as do you, who make their lives much more complicated than they need to be. When I am in their presence, I am often struck by how much more enjoyable life might be if they made the choice to see their experiences as simple lessons.

This lifetime of opportunities is our classroom. It's not as mysterious as many can make it seem. Life is never out to get us! It's quite manageable, really, with little more than a shift in perception.

I can't remember when I was initially introduced to the idea that experiences, no matter their content, are merely lessons awaiting recognition, but I know it gave me great peace, instantly. No one among us hasn't had at least one harrowing experience in the past. And if you are like I used to be, you no doubt thought your world was coming apart at the seams.

Even after coming to believe that our experiences are opportunities, we may need reminders of their positive value in the midst of a test. I don't mean to suggest that we can be completely at ease with every lesson the first time it beckons, but by choosing to believe that the lessons which bear my name were hand-picked by me, with the help of God, I can short circuit my ego's resistance. You can too.

Earlier, I said that I believe our reason for living is to heal our relationships and that the healing can't happen unless we are willing to acknowledge that a rupture exists. If we aren't sure there is a rupture, perhaps the best way to find out is to honestly assess how we feel when in the presence of each person who matters to us. If our feelings are not entirely peaceful, a rupture of some kind is present. What then?

Here is where this rule can best be applied. First, remember that a rupture is caused by the ego resisting to embrace a person or an idea, *a lesson,* that has sought recognition in us. Second, remember that every person and every idea that impacts our life is a part of the parcel of lessons we signed up for.

Additionally, remember that the choice of when to embrace the person or idea is always our own, but we must always finally embrace the person or idea. This is not as onerous as it may sound. After all, we are assured that every step can be taken in concert with our Higher Power.

Our lessons are never thrown upon us with no help for handling them. Never are we expected to face any situation, person, or new idea alone. We are not alone. Ever. We are always exactly where we need to be. And each opportunity that presents itself is vying for our attention, as another of life's lessons.

Perhaps it would be helpful to illustrate this rule with one of the experiences I recently had. As I've said earlier, I have been traveling on this Twelve Step recovery path for more than twenty-seven years. One might think that that many years of consistent meeting attendance would mean never veering off the path. How wrong that person would be, at least when it comes to my journey.

Although I have never had an alcohol or drug relapse since beginning recovery, I have had many emotional relapses, and they can be extremely devastating. In most cases they are not life threatening, but in the extreme, they can be. My most recent emotional relapse was a throwback to the always self-doubting person I was prior to recovery.

I was giving a report in a professional setting. I had been before this very group many times and I always enjoyed the process. I usually enjoy speaking before any kind of group, but while I was giving my report, the group's chair interrupted me by saying another person wanted to speak. I was stunned because this was not the general procedure, but what came next really surprised me. The other person gave the remainder of my report as though I wasn't even present.

I left the meeting truly distressed. I didn't understand what was behind this action on the part of either individual. I approached one of the men about it, and he seemed surprised, as though he hadn't realized what had transpired. He and I had worked very well together over the years, so I tried to simply accept his explanation and move on. But I kept going back to the incident, again and again.

I asked some of the other people present at the meeting if they noticed the odd way in which my report was taken over, and they had, but hadn't made much of it. The obsession was all mine! For days I relived the experience, and each time felt more unworthy and discounted. I began to imagine that others had been thinking, for a long time, that my reports were too long or too boring.

I received good support from some of the women in the group, but my feelings were still bruised. Finally, I remembered a line from one of my spiritual books, "Beware of the tendency to see yourself as unfairly treated." Bingo! That's exactly where I was. I was caught in the cycle of seeing myself as the center of the universe, and everything that was happening was happening *to* or *at me*.

Something had indeed happened at that meeting, but was it really intended to be a put-down, or might it have been nothing more than a lapse in judgment? If it was an intentional slight, does it really matter in the grand scheme of my life? I think not. However, not taking every situation so seriously is one of the lessons I have to learn again and again.

The best way for me to *relearn* this lesson (unfortunately, it happens more often than I want to admit) is to notice, quite intentionally, the other people on my path just as soon as I become self-absorbed. Whenever I become the focus of my attention, I am in trouble.

There are so many lessons we have to learn and then relearn all over again. It doesn't matter. God is not keeping score. Perhaps we are, but we shouldn't expect perfection. Progress is all we are asked to make, and willingness opens the door.

Touch Points

1. Lessons come once and then come again. Don't fret if you miss their first appearance.
2. Fear no lesson.
3. Each lesson is a building block.
4. The primary lesson is to forgive ourselves and others.
5. God is our partner through the process of every lesson.
6. No lesson will harm us.
7. Every lesson will enhance our understanding of the journey.
8. Every lesson is one we requested, whether we realize it or not.
9. Each lesson needs our acceptance so that we can offer our insights to another person who, not coincidentally, is journeying with us.
10. Our combined lessons are like the fingers of clasped hands.

❧ 1

Every Argument Is about Fear

The idea that every argument is about fear may seem a bit strong—it seemed so when I first considered it. But the longer I have ruminated about it, the truer it rings. Let me explain.

There is a school of thought that says that all human expressions reflect one of two feelings: love or fear. I am an adherent of this school, but I didn't grow up with it. On the contrary, in my family of origin, the expression of anger was predominant, and anger was never understood to be related, in any way, to fear. In my family, anger was a justified response to any situation that was out of someone's control. Whenever someone was not behaving the way my parents wanted them to, they became angry. In fact, even when neighbors or perfect strangers were not behaving according to my parents' standards, they got angry. A perfect example of this was in the political arena. My father got rageful almost daily at anything the other political party did or said. It didn't matter that he wasn't personally affected; he was right and they were wrong.

What I never understood at the time was that my parents were afraid! They were afraid of what others would think if we kids were out of control. They were afraid of where our misbehavior might take us. They were afraid of what it showed about them if we, or others, were not doing exactly as they expected. Fear ruled their lives.

Fear rules the lives of most people; my parents were certainly not the exception. Consider for a moment the most recent argument you were involved in, either as a participant or an observer. Can you see how fear instigated the scrimmage? One person perceived himself or herself as too vulnerable and weak in the situation, or possibly felt discounted and an argument ensued.

The myriad conflicts that occur around our globe demonstrate how fear develops into unnecessary tension that often gets played out in murderous ways. One country, one neighborhood, one ethnic group expresses anger, often resulting in a tragic outcome, because of fear that the other side is getting ahead, getting more of what each side wants.

Many of us sit back and shake our heads in dismay or sadness over the constant violence that erupts daily in places like Ireland, Israel, and Africa. "Why can't these people get along?" we lament. Generally the battles are over past occurrences, perceived as injustices, that keep reigniting because human nature keeps digging them up. Internally we scream, "Enough of this!" then stoop to fighting with a loved one over a situation that differs only in content, not in form.

Fear drives us to do irrational things. Why are we so afraid? Some would say that fear, at its base, is over the retribution we expect to face "on the other side," when we die, retribution that we fear is deserved. Others would say our fear is much more superficial, that we are simply afraid of looking inadequate in front of others so we prepare to do battle with anyone who disagrees with us. Our ego is merely protecting itself.

Personally, I think fear is caused by our unwillingness to recognize our similarities with others. We tend to so easily see our differences and then feel quite separate from those around us. When these feelings of separateness grow too great, we strike out at one another in fear rather than reach out in an attempt at intimacy that might be rebuffed.

My earlier statement that every expression is one of fear or one of love simplifies the world for me. It also signifies to me the appropriate reaction to any encounter. Meeting any unloving expression with an offer of love can change the dynamic of every single encounter we have.

We can change the world, you and I, by our willingness to change how we perceive and then react to the world around us. Margaret Mead said this so eloquently when she noted, "it may seem impossible to think that any one of us can make a difference in the world, but that, in fact, is the only thing that can make a difference in the world." Our assignment is crystal clear.

We can refrain from arguing. It's a decision, nothing more. It's not necessary to "be right" in every discussion one engages in. We have nothing *real* to fear, or lose, in any discussion with any person; therefore, we need not be argumentative.

When the other person we encounter is determined to have a battle, we can perceive them as filled with fear. We don't need to understand the reason for it. There doesn't need to be a rational explanation. It can simply be acknowledged, internally, and "forgiven." The discussion can then move on.

Believing that every argument is about fear and that every solution is an expression of love makes our experiences far more manageable. Upcoming events and past circumstances need not trouble us anymore.

We can be free—free of anxiety, free of uncertainty, free of the fear of not fitting in, free of the fear of what others might think, free of the fear of not being right. How we want to perceive the circumstances in our life is up to us. Seeing them as opportunities to express love is the benefit we receive by understanding that all of life is about love or fear.

Touch Points

1. No disagreement requires resolution, ever.
2. Recognizing the fear behind an attack allows us to feel compassion.
3. Fear is the opposite of love, but it is a cry for love nonetheless.
4. Where fear is present, separation is the root.
5. Seeing our oneness lessens our fear.
6. Fear inspires more fear.
7. Love nurtures more love.
8. Attacks are always based on fear.
9. Fear can be replaced by love with the assistance of our Higher Power.
10. Where two are fearful, only one needs to change.
11. Fear separates us.
12. Love connects us.
13. Silence softens us.

8

Struggles Are Opportunities in Disguise

For most of our lives, we have been engaged in conflicts, often times pointless, with both our loved ones and strangers. The slightest irritation can turn into an ugly fight. Our unwillingness to walk away can turn a small struggle into a far bigger matter.

Why is walking away from a disagreement so difficult? Every one of us can think of situations where we chose to engage in a discussion that we knew, sooner or later, would turn into an argument.

We probably had no idea that an engaged, perhaps even enraged, ego had taken over our thinking. All egos want to win whatever they are engaged in, be it a game, a casual discussion, a heated argument, or an all-out fight.

I spent most of my life, prior to recovery, exercising my ego. I fought with my dad as a youngster, both for myself and for my siblings, and fought with the boys in my neighborhood. I carried my need to dominate into my first marriage, then I fought my way through the marriage until it ended twelve years later.

I didn't know that the battleground was based on my fear and everyone else's. The very idea that fear was the root of every argument would have gotten an argument from me, in fact. I argued with others because of my certainty that I was right about whatever we were discussing. Of course, these others generally argued back because they were just as certain that they were right.

It takes some of us a long time to realize that *being right* is a matter of perspective. It takes even longer to understand that *being right* is irrelevant when it comes to the much larger picture of our lives.

People can learn to agree to disagree. They can learn to see disagreements as opportunities for growth. Those who can't give up the need to have the last word are letting a fearful ego rule their life. They move from one argument to another, seeking acceptance and approval for their opinions.

This brings us to the real substance of this rule. Every disagreement is an unexpected opportunity, clear and simple. It's an opportunity to express a different side of ourselves. It's an opportunity to forgive the adversary. It's an opportunity to forgive our need to judge others, and then to forgive our need to be right.

It has been far easier for me to see the opportunity in a conflict since I've understood that struggles are actually fears being manifested. I didn't grow up with this understanding and I lived the first few decades of my life without it. I was raised to see every conflict as an opportunity to wield power. I saw my father wield it and I imitated him with relish.

Seeing conflict as fear in disguise allows us to see the opportunity it presents us with as a gift in disguise. It's a gift many choose never to open, unfortunately. My recovery has often shown me the blessings inherent in this gift. To receive it, I have had to walk away from circumstances that angered me. I have had to pray for people I didn't really want to pray for. I have had to thank people for what our conflicts taught me.

In every struggle I willingly seized as an opportunity for growth, I found an unexpected benefit. I have come to believe that this will always be true, and it makes the potential for the unexpected gifts awaiting me all the more exciting.

When I was in early recovery, my sponsor shared a beautiful image with me. She suggested I see struggles as positive opportunities, as unexpected dancing lessons offered by God. I have treasured this advice ever since. Be grateful for your struggles. Enjoy your dancing lessons.

Touch Points

1. No struggle is too big to relinquish.
2. Each struggle holds an inherent lesson.
3. No struggle demands immediate resolution.
4. All struggles are blessings.
5. All struggles are opportunities to know ourselves better.
6. All struggles bring us closer to God if we allow them to.
7. All struggles allow us to give and receive forgiveness.
8. All struggles reflect fear.
9. No struggle can withstand the showering of love.

10. Every struggle can be interpreted as a time for rejoicing.
11. Every struggle gives us the opportunity to join with another.
12. Every struggle contains the solution within it.

❧ 9

Every Resolution Is a Loving Act

Resolution is the *coming together* of disparate opinions. Some might define it as the melding of minds that differ on a particular circumstance. Resolution means deciding to put aside our differences for the sake of the situation and the people affected. Being willing to resolve a disagreement is a choice that benefits everyone involved.

Relinquishing your opinion for the sake of resolution isn't easy. Most of us developed our opinions over many years of reading, thinking, and talking, and our opinions are dear to us. We may even think of them as friends if we have held them for a long time.

Because opinions—especially strong opinions—can define us, we might fear losing our identity if we deny them, ignore them, or fail to pay them proper homage when the opportunity to acknowledge them comes up.

Opinions generally dictate a person's behavior, unless the opinion holder has decided to keep it quiet for one reason or another. Occasionally this happens with ease, especially if someone is trying to make a new friend or form an alliance that might prove beneficial in the future.

Being willing to give up opinions, or at least set them

aside for the good of others, can be challenging. However, the spiritual path that has been guiding my recovery for many years now shows that a little willingness is enough to open the door so the rest of the willingness can get through.

What is really gained by "giving in," by relinquishing an opinion that has been a principle guiding one's life? Peace. Peace is gained through the decision to give in. It's a peacefulness that comforts everyone who is affected by the unresolved circumstance.

We have all been privy to situations where no one gave in. And we remember the tension, no doubt. We see countries refusing to give in all the time. Newspapers are replete with reports of this resistance, resulting in tense and violent conflicts worldwide.

I learned resistance well in my family of origin. Your family may have taught you to hold on to your opinion as well. But when one side or the other gives in, peace washes over all persons involved, a peace that is indefinable, and yet very perceptible.

We may not have learned to give in from our families of origin. In fact, this might have been the last place we could have learned it, and we may have to be the one to teach them the value of giving in. I can't say that I actually taught my family to give in, but I did help them understand what comprises a loving act. I did this, not by words, but by a change in my behavior. I learned to bow out, to walk away from an argument. After getting into recovery, I was able to walk away from many unnecessary arguments with my dad.

Coupling the "bowing out" with a smile changes the dynamic of the situation. Even more, it changes the people present to the situation in a profound way. This change can impact the future, too. What goes around comes around. We can't escape it, fortunately.

Every resolution is a loving act that never stops giving. It's an act that is multiplied again and again every time it is offered. As exemplified in the movie *Pay It Forward*, the good we do for others keeps working, and it will revisit us, too.

Remember that any act of goodness, whatever it is, will change the life of the recipient at the same time as it will change the experience of the giver. And the recipient, in turn, will change how life appears to someone else.

It's really so simple. A tiny decision, an even tinier action, can serve as the catalyst that changes how life is experienced by everyone, everywhere. Are you ready to demonstrate a loving act today?

Touch Points

1. A decision to walk away from an argument gets easier with practice.
2. Not having to win an argument is monumental.
3. Being willing to resolve a conflict contributes to world peace.
4. Being the first one to back away from a conflict sets a wonderful example.
5. Choosing peace over winning the argument is easier the second time we try it.
6. Demonstrating to others that opinions can be relinquished is a worthy action.

7. Our interactions and our opportunities to be bearers of peace are not coincidental.
8. This world needs every loving resolution possible. Are you willing to be a contributor for the good of us all?
9. Peaceful relationships will change every experience we have.

❧ 10
Make Every Response Gentle

I assume that every reader of this book is seeking guidance that might enhance his or her relationships. If that's true for you, I can't offer any guidance with more potential for doing so than this: make every response gentle. Responding gently to each and every remark will create a shift in how you are perceived, a shift in how you perceive the other person, and then a shift in the experience itself.

I think we all spend some time each day, even if only a minute or two, wishing a conversation had ended differently or a response had been given in a kinder, more thoughtful way. Most of us probably focus on the other person's behavior, not our own. But what we learn in recovery, or on any spiritual path, is that *change begins with me*.

This positive discovery means we can make our future different, very different, from our past. We are powerless over the actions and the responses of others, but we are not powerless over ourselves. How we receive or respond to another's actions or words is up to us.

Not being able to make someone else responsible for how we feel isn't very appealing when we first learn this idea. It's tempting to blame someone else for the difficult situations we find ourselves in. Unfortunately, blaming others stifles our growth, and it means our relationships are dishonest. There is no surer way to destroy a relationship than through blame.

Conversely, there is no surer way to enhance a relationship than through choosing to be gentle. The good news is that this choice is no more difficult than we make it. It can become a habit, a healthy habit, with a little willingness and practice on our part.

When our relationships feel tense, it's likely due to our own misperception. We have decided, no doubt unconsciously, to take the situation too personally.

Thinking the universe revolves around us is the poison that endangers our relationships. One solution is this: when we are having an experience that feels tense, disrespectful, or unfair, we can decide to respond to it in a gentle way. And we don't have to actually feel the gentleness, either. We can simply *choose* to act gentle.

Perhaps this seems dishonest, but I learned many years ago in recovery that "acting as if" can become the catalyst for real change. "Acting as if" serves as the blueprint for building a better foundation for all of our relationships. It doesn't mean we are ignoring what happened with the other person; it simply means we have made the choice to not react in a negative way. If we say anything at all, we will choose to say it gently.

Virtually no one escapes the need for building healthier relationships, particularly if they have ended up in a Twelve Step program. Most of us need to go back to the basics if we want successful relationships.

It's our good fortune that we have the opportunity to

re-create our relationships. They are our purpose for living. It's through relationships that we learn what we are here to do and can make our unique contributions to this life.

It's not surprising that we struggle in relationships. Being at odds with one another is part of the ego's learning curve. Tension doesn't make relationships any less valuable. We are drawn into relationship with individuals who have something specific to offer us, perhaps a difficult lesson or an opportunity for us to serve as their teacher.

There are no accidents. This is so easily forgotten, particularly when we are in the midst of a painful struggle with another person. It's not the struggle that matters, ever, even though it feels that way. It's the resolution. It's the coming together with another person to recognize our oneness, to honor the spirit within each of us. And we can do this best when we are being gentle with one another.

One of the best ways to practice this rule is to begin each day with a prayer, asking God, however you define God, to help you slow down your reactions to others. Then, before responding to any comment that has been made to you, pause for just a moment. In that pause, remind yourself to be gentle with your words. This simple act will transform each individual experience, and thus your entire day. If we practice this simple rule, we will be able to end each day with the certainty that we did no harm.

Touch Points

1. Being gentle doesn't mean being walked on.
2. Being gentle means using a quiet voice.
3. Being gentle means speaking slowly.
4. Being gentle means letting your heart be involved in your response.
5. Being gentle doesn't require that you agree with the other person.
6. Being gentle doesn't mean that you feel unheard.
7. Being gentle means letting your Higher Power have a stake in your response.
8. Responding to anger with gentleness changes the direction of the discussion while it changes both individuals.
9. Gentleness lowers anxiety while it raises the possibility for resolution.
10. Gentleness changes the dynamics of a situation.
11. Doing nothing more than being gentle in every interaction, for one day, will change one's life completely.
12. Being gentle once, makes being gentle twice easier.

❧ 11
We Must Heal the Issues That Derail Us

Have you noticed that changing relationship partners doesn't necessarily solve the sticky issues that emerge in a relationship? In fact, it never does. The issues, the lessons, or the opportunities that we have "signed up for" in this human experience will keep repeating themselves until we have learned what we needed to learn.

From my perspective, this is a very exciting realization, although, like you perhaps, I resisted it for the first few decades of my life. It's exciting to me now because it means that we have as many chances as we need, to eventually learn whatever it is we need to learn from one another in this human existence.

There is no shame in not learning the lesson the first time it was presented. When we learn the lesson is up to us; there is no time table. We are not in a race with anyone else in this school of life. God is not keeping track of our failed attempts.

We can, and many do, keep repeating the same lessons in relationships for years, resisting as long as possible the growth that the lesson offers. But the growth will wait for us. That's the fortunate news that we have been promised on this spiritual journey. We cannot escape what we need to learn. We must heal our relationships and ourselves.

No doubt most of us have a history of failed relationships. We can probably point to many issues that contributed to their failure. Maybe *he* wasn't sensitive enough, or *she* was too clingy. Whatever explanation we gave ourselves when the relationship failed seemed to satisfy us. But then the same behavior or issue surfaced in the next relationship. And then the next.

It's not the relationship partner that needs to change, regardless of how obnoxious or wrong the other person may be. We need to change. And nothing around us changes unless we change first.

I am not saying other people never need to improve their behavior, but the point is, we cannot focus on the other person. They will learn their specific lessons when they are ready. We can only attend to our own lessons and let go of theirs.

Being willing to change whatever needs to be changed *in us* isn't as difficult as it sounds. It's certainly a lot easier than trying to change someone else's behavior, which is impossible, at least for the long term.

Any relationship partner might be willing to change some things for a time but may revert back to the old behavior. We will not be able to stop this reversal, no matter what we say or do.

This brings the task of change to our doorstep, which is a good thing. It assures us that we can enjoy the success we desire and ultimately deserve. It doesn't assure us, though, that we will gleefully celebrate the task of changing. Change is seldom relished initially.

Most people can tolerate a lot of pain, and resisting change generally results in pain. We rarely surrender to change until we have tried every other way to cope with a troubling relationship.

My issues reared their ugly heads again and again. If it were not for the commitment I made to my spiritual path, a commitment that I continue to make on a daily basis, they would continue to hinder me. Now when the issues surface, as they still do, I seek another perspective.

Surprisingly, what's on the other side of the change we finally surrender to is freedom. Freedom to enjoy all our relationships. Freedom to stay in or leave any relationship. Best of all, freedom to accept responsibility for how the rest of our life and all of our relationships will evolve.

Healing what derails us in a relationship has more than one reward. It positively affects all of our other relationships, too. Healing one relationship contributes to the peacefulness of all relationships, everywhere, among all people. Unfortunately, the reverse is true as well.

The connectedness that exists between all members of the human community means that everything that happens to us will in time and in some way, impact all of us. The downside of this principle is that mean-spirited or violent behavior is also far-reaching in its effects. Remember, every time we willingly, or even not so willingly, heal one of our relationships, we are helping all relationships everywhere.

Knowing that the power rests with each one of us to

make this a better world is exhilarating and inspiring. Each day we need to ask ourselves, "Am I adding to the peace of the world today? What have I done to heal a relationship lately?"

Touch Points

1. There is really only one relationship to heal.
2. If we are at peace with ourselves, all relationships will be peaceful.
3. Any discomfort in a relationship tells us we have work to do.
4. It is only in relationship with others that we are presented with our lessons.
5. Healing one relationship will help all relationships.
6. When we let a relationship fester, we are contributing to the unpeaceful world that surrounds us.
7. World peace does rely on each one of us.
8. What we do to one, we do to all.
9. Whenever we help one person, we help all people.
10. We are examples for one another.
11. Wherever you are, you have a job to do.
12. Healing begins with me and you.

◜ 12
Be Humble and Honest

This rule was hinted at in the preceding one. No relationship is unaffected by the ripples in other relationships. When you attempt to heal one relationship, you positively affect all relationships. Likewise, when you behave humbly and honestly in any relationship, you contribute to the good health of all relationships.

Had I been introduced to this rule prior to joining a Twelve Step fellowship, I would have been confused. Being honest might have made sense to me, but I would have been stymied by the word *humble* and what it meant in the context of a relationship.

We learn in recovery that honesty with others is imperative if we are to live free of guilt and shame. Therefore, it is reasonable to expect a discussion of honesty as a rule for healing troubled relationships, but being asked to be humble may be a stretch for many of us.

My introduction to the idea of humility was when I read the list of Steps hanging on the wall at my first Twelve Step meeting in 1975. *Humbly asked God to remove our shortcomings,* it said. I understood nothing about Step Seven then. For that matter, none of the Steps resonated with me. I didn't think I had many shortcomings, but I was quite sure that most of the other people in my life did! In fact, that's why I went to an Al-Anon meeting. I intended to learn how I could change the behavior of the other people in my life who kept me in a constant state of anxiety. *They* had shortcomings, I was sure of it.

Fortunately for me, I stuck around and was directed to other Twelve Step meetings, too. The longer I went to meetings, the more aware I became about the need for humility, as well as honesty, in *all our affairs*.

I made the commitment to be honest in my relationships without much fanfare. However, it was much more difficult to follow through with it. Without even realizing it, I had been stretching the truth and minimizing little white lies for most of my life. I didn't see how far from the truth I had been living. I was in for a rude awakening.

Honesty is one of those principles that simply has no gray area. One is either honest or not. Period. It takes both willingness and practice, lots of it, to be absolutely honest. People often try to get away with shades of honesty or dishonesty. However, once committed to a Twelve Step program, the guilt of being dishonest weighs heavily on our relationships.

Honesty is so rewarding, but it also means accepting your "licks" for wrongs either spoken or done. No matter what the consequences are for our past dishonest behavior, accepting them will release us from the prison that has held us captive since the moment we told the lie.

Being honest with a mate impacts our dealings with colleagues, friends, and even strangers. *What we do to one of us, we do to all of us.* We are not separate beings. We are one. Even though we are separate in body, we are connected in spirit, and what is felt by one is felt by all. This includes the joys as well as the sadness, the laughter as well as the tears, the hope as well as the despair.

We find great hope in deciding to be absolutely honest and humble in all aspects of life. All our relationships will be more peaceful because we are free from the stress of lies and arrogance, and the miracle doesn't stop there. Everyone who benefits from our honesty and humility will be inspired to change how they behave in other relationships too. We will contribute to world peace with every humble and honest breath we take.

It may sound presumptuous to think we are affecting world peace with our daily actions, but indeed, we are. Because we are all connected in spirit, our thoughts, our actions, our reactions, and every single one of our prayers, impact all of us. No thought, no action, no prayer goes unheard by the *whole.* Even if we think people are not listening, the message gets registered in spirit.

It's easy to live a less stressful life. The hard part is deciding to do what is necessary to get there. Throughout the day, we need to ask ourselves: Can I be trusted, absolutely, to be honest in a loving way? Am I listening to my inner voice? It will always keep us humble.

There is an additional, very significant reward for being more honest and humble in our relationships. Simply, we will like ourselves better! Most of us complicated our lives by being neither honest nor humble, and our predicaments grew worse. We seldom added to the resolution, and all parties walked away angry, hurt, or both. It wasn't easy to like ourselves in those instances.

We never have to experience situations like that again! We can walk away from every encounter with a clear conscience and a light heart, knowing that our presence made it more peaceful. That's an incredibly exhilarating realization. Do you share my excitement?

There is no better time than right now to make the decision that will change the rest of your life. The decision is small yet very profound. Are you ready? Let's think this through together: *We are ready to live each moment of today honestly and humbly. We are ready and willing to let God, as we understand God, choose our words, our thoughts, and our actions. We are ready to make our contribution to the whole. Let us begin.*

Touch Points

1. Making the decision to be honest is the first step.
2. Any attempt at honesty is a good start.
3. Willingness to listen to and follow our inner voice will save us from dishonest behavior.
4. As with all good traits, we must practice honesty and humility.
5. Being humble means being willing to accept our shortcomings and learn from them.
6. Acknowledging the importance of all the "travelers" on our path is a humbling experience.

7. Changing our behavior in one relationship makes changing it in all relationships easier.
8. We need to demonstrate honest, humble behavior.
9. Every time we treat another person honestly, we change his or her life along with our own.
10. Seeking God's direction in all things will ensure that we respond to our relationships both honestly and humbly.

❧ 13
Avoid Judging Others

Does "avoid judging others" mean that we must never make a judgment about an experience with another person? Not exactly. It's certainly okay to decide that we don't want to have future experiences with certain people. In fact, it might be in our best interest to make that decision.

We can make choices about what to do or where to go based on our personal judgment of any number of circumstances we have already experienced. But it is never appropriate to sit in judgment of another person's perspective or behavior. Those things are between that person and his or her Higher Power. Let's never forget, we are not anyone's Higher Power.

When we don't live by a clear and complete commitment to this rule, our thinking can get sloppy. Before long, we find ourselves stewing about people and circumstances that are none of our business. The truth of the matter is, no one else's behavior is our business!

It's not as difficult as it may seem to stop judging others. We can make a habit of healthy thinking and acting—we've certainly made habits of bad behaviors and bad thinking patterns in the past. The drill is the same either way. Practice, practice, practice!

One of the benefits of not judging others is personal freedom. We likely haven't considered the amount of time we devote to harboring ill thoughts about others on a daily basis. We spend far more time sitting in judgment than exploring our creativity or in fostering good notions about the people who share our journey.

Deciding to take charge of our thoughts and choosing not to harbor any unloving or unkind thought about another person shifts our perspective in a profound way. Nothing about our life will seem the same. Indeed, the lives of those who are sharing our journey will be positively affected by this decision as well.

We are creatures of habit: we have heard this thousands of times. What we haven't heard as often, but what is equally true, is that we have the personal power—every one of us— to decide what *kind* of creature we are going to be. Doing what we always did may feel comfortable in the short run, but if it creates tension or conflict, shouldn't we consider doing something else?

That something else is simple. For some, it might even seem too simple. If your life has been anything like mine, you didn't get here by following simple directions for a happy life. Most of us got to the point of reading a book like this because we didn't do anything the simple way. We complicated our lives, often with alcohol and other drugs, and always with bad relationships, because we were desperately in search of control of something, anything. But whatever we were after eluded us.

The past is done. It has no control over us—none that we don't willingly give it, that is. The future will be whatever we choose to make it when we get there. Right now, the present offers us every opportunity we have been prepared for.

We can appreciate our opportunities and cherish them as blessings, or we can judge them and the people involved and miss the lessons offered to us. The choice is ours. It has always been ours. It will always be ours. We know from the pain of the past that bad choices have bad results. And now we also know that the opposite is true too: *good* choices have *good* results.

Are you facing this day and the many people and experiences that have been "prepared" for you with a clear and open mind? If so, you will discover how exhilarating life can be when you are free from unnecessary judgment. This journey may take you to places you never imagined going. It will certainly bring you many moments of pleasure and peace. Now go forth with eager anticipation and leave the work of judging to God.

Touch Points

1. Making the decision not to judge others is a choice.
2. It is a choice that one can make repeatedly every day.
3. After making this choice a few times, it gets easier.
4. Making this choice feels freeing and good.
5. Judgment restricts us as much as it harms others.
6. Our growth depends on our willingness to love and forgive. Judgment prevents both.

7. Every time we judge another person, we are judging ourselves.

8. Freeing one person frees all of us.

9. Those people we unfairly judge are on our path intentionally.

10. We have come together to learn and to teach. Judgment prevents both.

11. It is our work to love, to help, to forgive. Only when we practice these acts will we know peace.

14

Begin Each Day by Asking,
What Can I Bring to My Relationships?

No one's day is free from interruptions. Each day presents many possibilities for rudeness and hostility. Often, our day gets going before we are really ready for it to begin. Perhaps an unexpected phone call wakes us up or there has been a power outage and our alarm doesn't ring. When our day begins like this, we are primed for saying things we don't really mean and doing things that are not in the best interest of ourselves or others.

There is one way we can be certain that the day begins the way we want it to. We can take a few minutes shortly after rising to be quiet with ourselves. In that quiet space, we can ask, what can I bring to my relationships today? Taking this time allows our Higher Power to center us and help us develop the attitude of gratitude that will guarantee we will relate to others with love and kindness. If we follow this plan, we'll have a smooth journey all day long.

Having a spirit of gratitude throughout a single day will be transforming, both for ourselves and the others sharing each experience. This is no exaggeration. Being grateful for expected and unexpected experiences will give them a meaning they could not have otherwise had.

Gratitude, as a feeling, seems almost mind-altering; some might even say intoxicating. It excites the spirit and honors every person present too. Only constant practice will convince the nonbeliever.

Fortunately, I have come to believe that gratitude is a decision. It is fortunate because it means I have complete control over how I feel. I may not be able to prevent certain outcomes, nor can I decide how another person might respond to the circumstances lying before us, but I know my own reactions won't create unnecessary complications.

This is a very powerful awareness. It's not one I had when I first entered recovery. In fact, before recovery I was distraught most of the time because I couldn't keep my problems from escalating. I felt very little joy, and I certainly didn't feel grateful for my life or the people in it. On the contrary, I was quite certain that if I had a new set of circumstances, a new group of friends, and most of all, a new husband, I would be problem free. When I had all that, maybe I could feel grateful.

Many of these things did change for me after I found a Twelve Step program. However, the joy I thought I deserved still eluded me until I discovered the meaning and the usefulness of gratitude.

Nothing can really defeat us if we remember the power we have over our own minds. We simply don't need to hang on to any negative thought. No matter how angry we might feel about a situation, we don't have to continue feeling angry. It might take a concentrated effort to shift our perception, but it can be done.

What a gift! We should not underestimate its value or

power. The promise it implies is that nothing about today or any future day can have a result that doesn't meet with our willing (though not necessarily eager) acceptance.

Do we choose to bring to the table our kindness, our gratitude, and our generous spirit every day? Hardly. But if we can do so every other day or even once a week, we will make our lives and the lives of those we journey with so much more pleasant. Also, any day we start out on the wrong foot can be salvaged just as soon as we shift our attitude to one of gratitude. We are never stuck with our initial mindset if it isn't bringing us joy.

The big question is: what do we do with the many negative attitudes and situations that still claim our attention? I have learned through the Twelve Steps that my Higher Power can help me seek a grateful perspective. Thus, I am assured of being able to change my experiences. By changing my mind, I change my life. The key is the choice—it is always ours.

I'd like to share an additional tool for changing a negative mindset, one that is frequently suggested in Twelve Step recovery rooms. Before turning off the light when you crawl into bed at night, make a list of the things that occurred throughout the day that you feel grateful for. Think upon these things as you wander off to sleep. What we let linger in our minds multiplies. Happy dreams.

❧❧

Touch Points

1. Take a minute to seek God's help and perspective before doing anything.
2. Seeing the good in a situation is a decision.
3. Seeking the good ensures that you will bring your better self to each experience.
4. Experiencing gratitude can become a habit.
5. Be wary of negative attitudes, because they too can become habits.
6. Make a gratitude list daily.
7. Make this list even if you can name only one thing you were grateful for.
8. Meditate upon this list while going to sleep.
9. Reread this list upon waking.
10. Reread the previous days' lists.
11. Practice silence if you are feeling negative about a situation.
12. Practice changing your mind when you are feeling negative.

ஃ 15

Start Your Day with God

"Start your day with God" seems almost too trite to suggest as a rule, yet good habits are hard to form. Personal experience has taught me how easy it is to forget my Higher Power when I am preparing for the day's activities. Generally speaking, if I begin my first task before taking a few moments to think about God, I get ahead of myself and begin to project into the outcome and beyond. Getting off on the wrong foot is far easier than I like to admit.

What does it mean to start the day with God? The answer varies for each of us. I begin my day reading some spiritual passages with my husband and quietly reflecting on them, sometimes sharing our views and other times just sitting in silence. Closing my time with the Serenity Prayer reminds me that it is God's will, not mine, that I need to honor.

This is such a simple action and requires so little time that it's hard to believe I skip it some mornings. But I do, and the repercussions are often quite swift. I certainly don't believe that God is keeping score and sends me a problem as payback for neglecting our time together, but I do believe that when I forget to think first of God, my subsequent actions are less considerate, less gentle, and then others react accordingly.

Thinking of God first in the morning immediately softens my outlook and has a profound impact on the way my entire day unfolds. It's almost as though I can see the people and experiences that are part of my destiny through God's eyes.

Throughout my day, I sometimes get off track, even when I do my morning ritual, but I know that I can return to the Serenity Prayer and calm will return instantly. This generally doesn't happen without my invitation though.

I have tried to incorporate into my day a subtle but constant awareness of God's presence while I interact with my partners on this journey. It empowers me to be my better self, and it removes whatever feelings of isolation and separation I may have had.

I learned long ago that the disease I suffer from, alcoholism, loves isolation all too much. At Twelve Step meetings, we often say, "We are in very poor company when we are alone in our heads." I know, I have the scars to prove it. Even though we are never really alone, we do manage to block out the awareness of God all too easily. At least that's true for me.

Remembering that God is always present during every moment of my journey, whether I am conscious of it or not assures me that the outcome will be far gentler than when I let my own ego assume the role of God.

There is nothing difficult about deciding to begin each day by acknowledging God. Unfortunately, many of us think we should not have to remake this decision once it has been made, but that's simply not how life works. We have to remake many important decisions on a daily basis; praying is just one of them.

Forgetting God's constant presence is just too easy without some prodding. I am so grateful for my frequent reminders from sponsors and friends. My relationships with all people have reaped the benefits. Conversely, all of my relationships suffer every day that I forget to take some time with God. How easily we add to our difficulties when we forget to remember God!

Touch Points

1. Upon arising, think first of God.
2. As you ponder any thought or action, try to discern what God would have you think or do.
3. Make a habit of "taking God with you" wherever you go.
4. Conversing with God in your mind is not very difficult if practiced.
5. While doing any task, the complex as well as the simple, become aware of God's presence.
6. Remember, God never leaves you.
7. If you are experiencing any anxiety, you have forgotten to remember God's presence.
8. God is everywhere. Take notice.

ॐ 16
Choose Once Again

I needed some explanation when I was first introduced to the idea of choosing once again. But I have come to treasure it as a gift that never quits giving to my relationships with others. Simply speaking, here's how it works: When anyone, anywhere, does or says anything that you are tempted to respond to in a negative way, don't respond. Choose again.

Deciding to think before making any response allows us to choose less hurtful words or actions. This doesn't mean we have to deny that someone has done something distasteful or demeaning, but it allows us to respond from a higher plane of consciousness.

Responding in kind by being mean-spirited toward the other person hurts our self-perception every bit as much as it hurts the other person. The damage isn't limited to just the two of us, either. Every person we are in relationship with will be affected by the way we handle any of the difficult circumstances that are a normal part of daily life.

Earlier I stated that what we do to one, we do to all. This idea is reflected here as well. Responding in any way that's disrespectful to any other person on our path will ultimately hurt others as well. Thus, consider your response and when necessary, choose again before acting.

One of the immediate benefits of *choose once again* is freedom from all arguments. By stopping ourselves from making any response before thinking it through, we allow ourselves time to decide to make only those responses that will enhance whatever outcome we desire. We will thereby avoid an argument as well.

Try this for a day: When anyone makes a comment to you that you instantly want to snarl at, take a deep breath, smile, keep quiet for a moment, then say, "I am sorry you feel that way," or, "I am sorry you are having a bad day," or, "Is there something you would like from me right now?"

Saying these words with a respectful tone might diffuse the anger. Anger often camouflages the fear that is underlying an interaction, and fear usually triggers any tense situation. Fear motivates people to say and do things they feel extremely uncomfortable with or even ashamed of, such as snapping back at someone in anger.

Being willing to do our part to enhance our relationships has great rewards. Not only do we feel better in the moment when we have been able to lessen the tension in an encounter, but all of us feel the ripple effect. Most of us forget this payoff, but the interconnectedness of all members of the human community is a reality.

How we act is our choice. From this moment on. Would you like to make a contribution that will benefit all human kind? Do you want to foster peace throughout the world? If your answer is yes, your choice is simple. Choose again when the response you are about to make to anyone isn't kind.

Touch Points

1. Taking a moment to reconsider a response can change the tone of every conversation.
2. Every one of us is an emissary for peace if we want to be.
3. Not responding is better than responding with anger.
4. A genuine smile can often diffuse an ugly situation.
5. A deep breath can alter our perspective.
6. One resolution benefits many struggles.
7. Every peace-filled moment manifests in kind.
8. Changing the world is not our job. Changing our mind is.
9. Every changed mind, every peaceful mind, adds to the changing of the world.
10. Choice is all we have. Choice is all we need.
11. Choose wisely. Each one of us is affected by it.

17

Always Ask, Would I Rather Be Peaceful or Right?

Always asking myself whether I'd rather be peaceful or right is the greatest bit of shorthand advice for creating peaceful relationships that I have ever come across. *A Course In Miracles*, a spiritual book familiar to many people in Twelve Step programs, along with AA and Al-Anon, deserves the credit for this suggestion.

Before engaging in any confrontational behavior, before trying to force someone to do life *your way*, or before responding to someone in a way that might trigger a negative response, ask yourself: Would I rather be peaceful or right? Let your answer dictate the substance of your response.

Asking ourselves this question before beginning a conversation or formulating a response allows us the opportunity to make a clear choice about what our input should be. In certain discussions, a person may not prefer to be peaceful, and that's okay.

It's our human nature, or some might call it our momentary insanity, to want to stir up trouble once in a while. However, my angry outbursts or retorts never leave me feeling very satisfied. Each of us has to evaluate for ourselves the so-called "good" that might come from choosing to be *right* instead of peaceful.

I've mentioned that I grew up in a very argumentative family. My parents, particularly my dad, simply had to be right about everything. From music to politics, we were not allowed the freedom to have an opinion different from his. That's all it took for me to cry foul, again and again. Even those times that I more or less agreed with him, I argued. It was the principle, after all. What a tiresome situation I contributed to for many decades. How grateful I am that I became willing to respond differently before my father died.

No doubt most of us have worsened a relationship by not choosing a moment's peace over the transparent need to be right or to have the last word. The desire to control a situation or another person is just too great for many people. The occasional time we manage to wrest control from someone else, seduces us into trying it again the next time we are in a similar circumstance. And the dance goes on.

Complicating our lives by these frequent, unnecessary and meaningless arguments is much too common. Unfortunately, this scenario manifests on the larger world screen too. The millions of individuals who are in a constant state of agitation resulting in nonstop, argumentative discourse with their friends and neighbors are inadvertently helping to create the disharmony that exists all over the world. One conflict adds to another, exponentially.

We have all known people who seemed to fuel their very being by arguing, ad nauseum, over meaningless principles or circumstances. I once had a neighbor like this. He read the daily paper first thing every morning and then headed out to do battle with anyone who might not agree with his assessment of the leading news stories. It was like a game, his chosen hobby perhaps.

People like this are seldom in search of peace. For them, life is a contest; being right and being in control are the reasons they savor being alive. To them, peacefulness might be synonymous with boredom. Best we stay out of their way.

However, if we are in their space and need to respond to them, we can do so without adding fuel to their fire. Our contribution can be kind, thus offering a breath of peace to the specific situation and to the rest of the world. By not engaging in their battle, we will maintain our own balance, our own sense of well-being. We can simply decide to let them *be right* (or think they are right at least) and go on our merry way.

The beauty of this rule, like many of the other rules, is that we are making a contribution to the greater good of humankind each time we practice it. The decision is ours and can be made within the context of every conversation, each situation, and all experiences. No one is keeping score of how many times we break or adhere to the rules. But the tenor of our lives will reveal the choices we have made.

I have come to appreciate the personal empowerment that comes with not getting pulled into someone else's drama. For years it was second nature to let everybody's drama become my own. But I am free at last! Every time I make the better choice, I am free. And what sweet freedom it is.

Al-Anon principles and *A Course in Miracles* have certainly helped me learn how to choose peace over the need to be right, but real success depends on practice, practice, practice. I feel blessed that I have had the willingness during these many years in recovery to practice choosing peace when my first inclination was to spout off, to make myself heard, to "win" the argument at all costs. Old habits die hard, and new ones require work and patience, but they can find a home within if we make a space for them.

While writing this book, I have realized more than once how lucky I am to have the disease of alcoholism. Without it, I simply would not have come to cherish the many "rules" I have chosen to share with you here. I can even say without fear of contradiction that I would not have been introduced to these ideas had I not been in the kind of pain that led me to AA and Al-Anon.

My gratitude is profound, but I also realize that *chance has played no part in my life*. We are always where we need to be. By learning these ideas and sharing them with you I am fulfilling God's will for my life.

My sincere prayer is that you will decide to choose peace in your life today. Choosing peace over agitation has paid me many dividends, and will pay you many too. This world of ours needs as many infusions of peace as we can give it.

TOUCH POINTS

1. Choosing peace can become a habit.
2. Not engaging in arguments is very freeing.
3. Being right is a matter of perspective.

4. Choosing peace reduces tension.

5. Being right doesn't feed one's soul. Opting to be peaceful does.

6. Every choice to be peaceful adds to the peace of mankind.

7. It's a simple decision to walk away from an argument.

8. Each time we walk away, we feel greater empowerment.

9. Each time we walk away, we set an example for someone else.

10. Each time we walk away, we are helping to change the world.

11. A peaceful world requires peaceful people. Can you be counted on?

❧ 18
Chance Plays No Part in Our Lives

When I was first introduced to the idea that chance plays no part in our lives, I was very uncomfortable, even a bit paranoid. I didn't like the suggestion that every difficult experience I had was part of my destiny. It seemed to mean that I had no free will and that God had not protected me from dangerous situations.

A sponsor in my early recovery helped me see that the many harrowing experiences I had survived, *with God's help,* would become the material for the many books I have written. The experiences bore my name. I did have free will, she said, and I was allowed to choose my responses, but the experiences were specifically mine to live through, just as these books were mine to write.

The absence of chance in my life helps me appreciate the tapestry my life has been weaving for decades. It gives me solace to know that I was always where I needed to be. We always are where we need to be.

When the experience was painful, like my first marriage was, it was hard to accept that I *needed* to be in it. However, the lesson I was there to learn didn't have to consume twelve years of my life; it could have been learned more quickly.

My inability to make healthier choices throughout that time span slowed my learning curve, but the information I needed to know waited for me. That's the good news. It will always wait for us. And when we are ready to understand it, we will.

No matter what experience we are having, it has been selected for us. We have participated in the selection, in fact; we simply don't remember our involvement in the selection process. The form of the experience can vary. It might be a marriage, a job, a friendship, even an accident of some kind. But the content, the substance of what we need to learn, is specific and unwavering.

Believing that it's the content of the lesson that counts, not the form it comes in, gives me comfort. It makes the unexpected experiences, particularly those experiences that trigger fear in me, more tolerable. In other words, it's never the specific relationship that matters. It's the opportunity to expand my understanding of love and forgiveness that matters in the end.

Truly knowing what love and forgiveness mean and being able to offer them to others is why we are here. I am absolutely convinced of this. I have even come to embrace the idea that the family I was born into was selected by me, with the help of my spiritual guides, because of the opportunities inherent in my family to learn about love and forgiveness.

This idea frightened me when I was first introduced to it, but now it gives me immeasurable comfort. Chance has never played a part in my life. Never, ever. And that's what helps me look to the many tomorrows in my life, knowing that the same will always be true. What I need to experience and know will come to me by design.

I think we all have spiritual guides. They nudge us along, comfort us when we're afraid, remove the obstacles we don't really need to experience, and fine-tune the lessons so that we can accept them. We can walk away anytime we want to—temporarily. But the guides will remain and so will the lessons. We have no choice but to finally learn our spiritual lessons. Only the timetable is ours. And that's quite reassuring, don't you think?

Touch Points

1. Worry is a choice, never a necessity.
2. What we need to know and experience will always surface.
3. We have participated in the selection of our lessons.
4. Our experiences are never happenstance.
5. We cannot refuse a lesson we need to learn forever.
6. Our lessons will wait for us.
7. We will repeat the past until we learn from it.
8. We are always in the right place at the right time.
9. We cannot escape our destiny. Thank God!
10. Those travelers on our path are in their right place too.
11. Be comforted by the knowledge that all is as it should be.
12. Be peaceful. Life is perfect as it is.

∾ 19
Every Encounter Expresses Love or Fear

This is one of my favorite rules. It clarifies everything that is happening around me, so I am seldom mystified by anyone's comments or behavior. I simply remember that either love or fear is the underlying message, regardless of how it seems at first.

When love is the message, it's fairly easy to recognize. Loving expression comes in the form of words, unrequested favors, flowers, notes, and countless other unexpected courtesies. One thing common to all loving messages is they never hurt.

Fear wears myriad disguises, and many of them do hurt. Fear is often masked by anger, which manifests itself in overt rage, violent actions, swearing and yelling, or covert snipes. The covert forms are the most common. Snide comments, subtle or obvious put-downs, ugly gossip, and derision of any kind are indications of unacknowledged, covert fear. But silence can mask fear too.

We can seldom do anything about the specific fear that others express. We can, however, decide to not let their fear assume control of our own reaction (unless we are being attacked bodily, in which case we need to remove ourselves from the setting at once).

When we are able to recognize the many forms of fear, we can respond with love, compassion, and understanding. Giving a thoughtful response to another person can serve as an important catalyst for a significant change in both the other person and the experience itself.

Refusing to let someone else's expression of fear breed more fear is a decision we can make as many times as the opportunity presents itself. I can assure you that it is very empowering to treat someone's expression of fear with detachment, even acceptance—better yet, kindness. Not resorting to a mean-spirited response heals us in multiple ways.

We may wonder why there is so much fear present in so many of us worldwide. Psychologists and psychiatrists have been trying to answer this question for millions of patients since the time of Freud. Members of the clergy have tried to offer solace and answers to their parishioners too. And still, fear abounds. The many wars between nations evidence how fear multiplies on a universal level. After twenty-seven years in recovery, I have formed a conclusion about fear that satisfies me: Fear overcomes us and then undermines our very being when we feel separate, alone, and disconnected from God and our fellow human beings.

In a moment of imagined *separation*, we become self-conscious and self-absorbed, and we assume we are less worthy than every other person we encounter. We want to hide out and yet be noticed. When this happens to nations of people, wars start.

Most of us dread this feeling of separation and isolation so much that when it comes, we get angry and want to blame someone else. The fear of feeling separated drives us to say and do things that we'd never do when in our *right mind*. The *right mind,* the mind that knows it is connected to God, always knows we are not alone; it always knows we are never forgotten by God.

We often deny the right mind's input when we most need it. The insanity of choosing fear over faith, and thus over love too, is unexplainable, but it happens. Repeatedly. Fortunately there is a simple solution. We can choose to change our perspective.

We've already discussed how changing our perspective is little more than a decision. The best way to tell if it's time for a shift is to ask yourself, "How am I feeling?" If you can't answer "love-filled," it's time to change your mind, to shift your perspective.

Not responding with fear is the best gift we can give to every person we encounter. Giving love where healing is needed is what heals. This decision is neither mysterious nor difficult, and it calls to us daily. It's the sum and substance of a changed world. As anthropologist Margaret Mead said so many years ago, the world changes one person at a time. It's time for each of us to do our part.

Touch Points

1. Love is more easily recognized than fear.
2. Fear is the more prevalent expression we observe in others.
3. A loving response is the right response.
4. Responding with kindness is never a mistake. It helps to change the world, one person at a time.
5. Everyone is looking for love.
6. Our fear can be relieved by remembering God's presence.
7. Remembering *who we really are* makes the expression of love far easier.
8. We can shift from feeling fear to feeling love in a moment's time.
9. Every loving expression we offer comes back to us.
10. Every fearful expression is a cry for help that we can answer.
11. Make no response that wouldn't please God.
12. Make every response honorable.

❧ 20
When in Conflict, Seek a Shift in Perspective

Seeking a shift in perspective is a rule that most of us can apply dozens of times a day. Conflicts simply happen. Fortunately, most conflicts are minor and quite often they exist entirely within one's mind. They can happen at the grocery store when someone gets ahead of us in line, or in traffic when someone cuts in front of us. They can happen during the many conversations we engage in throughout the day, too.

A conflict doesn't have to be a big deal for us to let it take over our emotions; it doesn't even have to be verbalized. Too frequently, we let minor disagreements turn into major setbacks in a relationship simply because we choose to exaggerate the conflict's meaning to the rest of our life.

There is a simple solution for freedom from all conflicts: *Take Charge*. Take charge of what is in your mind. Take charge of what you dwell on. When you are not experiencing happiness, take note of what's in your mind, discard it, and shift your perspective. What we envision, we experience. Always.

The insidious aspect of any conflict is that it is not inviolate. It binds itself to every experience it possibly can. Entire days can be affected because our minds become contaminated by what we chose to harbor there.

We don't need to let conflicts assume control over our emotions. With practice, we can learn to resist giving any conflict power over our minds, even when the conflict is major. Only then can we be certain the conflict won't take charge of our actions too. If the conflict exists solely in our minds, only one person is affected—us. But we generally voice our conflicts and unleash a tidal wave of emotions in the process.

I scoffed when I first heard I could save myself from innumerable bad feelings and a host of resentments by shifting my perspective. It sounded like a set-up for a major denial of my feelings, which would mean I was willingly letting others walk all over me.

I had learned in the early '70s the value of asserting myself. I let other people know exactly how I felt and the details of each opinion I had. My often unrestrained behavior helped destroy more than one relationship, and it caused a great deal of injury to my familial relationships too.

Until I got into recovery, I resisted changing how I behaved in relationships. But I began to notice that the people I admired seemed a lot more peaceful than me, and I got curious as to how they did it. I loved being around people who seldom got angry. They seemed unaffected by any turmoil, and they didn't gossip or complain about the actions of others. And when I complained, they generally remained quiet, neither agreeing nor disagreeing.

It was only after I was able to see the *power* in their way of relating to the world that I was ready to experiment with doing it their way. This meant taking control of my mind. What a surprise was in store for me—and what a gift. Now I am more willing to see what "my mind is up to" and then make the decision to change my perspective.

I don't intend to claim that I am always at peace, but I actually have very few conflicts with others now. I sometimes have to reframe how I see a situation or take a deep breath and disengage from a nonproductive conversation, but I can do these things quite easily and I feel so much better for making the choice.

I can also choose to say, "Perhaps you are right," even when I don't really think so. I don't consider this dishonesty: I am just acknowledging the other person's right to have an opinion. Nothing is gained by most conflicts and so much can be lost over a meaningless argument.

The smallest actions can result in the biggest miracles. There is not much that is smaller than a smile, a nod, and an unspoken thought when the thought held in the mind was hateful and unnecessary. The next step is to let the thought slip away. Lives are changed every day by making this decision and taking this action. Consider it. What is won is extraordinary.

Touch Points

1. We can change the contents of our minds instantly.
2. Shifting our perspective becomes easier with practice.

3. Nothing needs to upset us ever again when we utilize this power to change our mind.

4. Shifting our perspective empowers us in awesome ways.

5. We cannot control others. We can control ourselves.

6. Conflicts need two or more participants to continue. We need never be one of the two.

7. We always have the opportunity to practice shifting our perspective.

8. There are no accidents. Conflicts are our opportunities for growth.

9. Being willing to see differently is all we need to have a different perspective.

10. Our lives will change dramatically if we become willing to change our minds.

11. Each positive shift in our perspective positively impacts the people around us.

12. When enough people choose to shift their negative perspectives, relationships around the world will change.

13. One positive shift in perspective is the beginning to a better life.

⌘ 21
Interpretations Determine Feelings

We choose how to interpret every situation that unfolds in our life. The interpretations we make generally reflect past experiences, even when those experiences are very much unrelated. The feelings that follow, then, match the past rather than the present.

We are creatures of habit, so we often restrict our vision regarding the many situations engaging us. We look through the same old tired eyes at the present circumstances. Even though we need a fresh, unbiased interpretation of every situation, we seldom seek one. Often, the tiniest element of the present circumstance brings us back to an earlier experience and we fail to see what's actually before us. What happened in the past gets replayed yet again.

When we repeatedly misinterpret what lies before us, we fail to gather the new information that reaches out to us for our growth and edification. The opportunity to learn each lesson will come again, of course, but our learning curve is lengthened every time we see the past rather than the present and our negative feelings gain strength.

The interpretations we too easily make reflect, and then continue to feed, the persona we have grown accustomed to. This isn't always bad, but personal growth requires that we be willing to stretch, to change, to let go of both the good and the bad experiences of the past.

Staying stuck in the past can only work if everyone else in our life stays stuck too. This is unlikely, no matter how hard we may fight against their changing. When the significant people in our life begin to change and we don't, the pain of our staying the same can only lead to the demise of the relationship. Some relationships may end, but if the lessons we needed to learn from them have not been learned, a similar relationship will take us hostage again. Of this we can be certain.

I used to be disheartened every time I realized I was repeating an old pattern or being reintroduced to an old lesson, one I had assumed I was finished with. Backsliding, I called it, and I felt ashamed. But when I heard my experience repeated by others, I came to understand that there is no shame in relearning our lessons. We only need to let go of our resistance to the reeducation process.

Repeating old stuff means we haven't yet learned what we need to learn, but I realize now that there is no time limit on these lessons. They simply deserve a fresh perspective, and when we give them another look, one that's unbiased, they will edify us and trouble us no more. The old feelings will go with them, too.

A long time ago a friend told me, rather exasperatedly after listening to my whining one too many times, that feelings are not facts! We determine them. We hang on to them. We rehash them. Over and over. And then we wonder why our lives stay the same.

She also wisely said, "Nothing changes when nothing changes." Her best suggestion to me was, "Get over it!" I love passing this on to others, particularly to those who refuse to let the past be over. We have all been there.

From years of being on a spiritual path, I have learned and relearned that the change agent for my life is me. How lucky that that is true for us all. We need nothing but our own resolve to change our life. *That, and a little help from God.*

First we need to be willing to look again at the experience before us. Then we must decide to actually see whatever is there to be seen from unbiased eyes. We must discard the old interpretation in order to accept the new interpretation.

This process is how we ready ourselves for our next set of experiences. They will present themselves when we have prepared the way for them. There is a rhythm to how our lives unfold. We can get in step with the rhythm just as easily as we get out of step. Where we place our attention is the deciding factor.

Being on a spiritual path makes it possible for us to change our perception, thus our life, at will. No interpretation is forced on us. No experience controls us unless we decide to let it, and no specific feeling is demanded of us. For every one of us, God is never more than a tiny thought away, and with God's help, all circumstances will become blessings.

Those of us who walk a spiritual path know this truth, and we have the opportunity to share this knowledge with others every day. Not just our tiny world, but the larger world that claims all of us, can profit from what we have come to understand and celebrate. There are no accidents. Wherever we are, we have a message to give as well as one to receive. Let's listen up!

Touch Points

1. Thoughts manufacture feelings. Thoughts can be changed.
2. Our lives change when our thoughts change.
3. We repeat old patterns when we hang on to old thoughts.
4. Feelings cannot control us.
5. Feelings have only the power we give them.
6. We can see familiar situations in new ways.
7. Fresh interpretations offer new understandings.
8. We cannot grow if we do not change our interpretations.
9. Nothing changes when nothing changes.
10. We determine our present as well as our future.
11. We are responsible for taking charge of our own life.
12. How we move forward is up to us.
13. How we experience each moment is in our hands.

✥ 22
Every Encounter Is Holy

This rule charts a course to follow if we decide to accept it as *the truth*. Never again will we be able to so easily dismiss anyone's remarks or actions if we view every encounter as a holy encounter.

Let's consider in greater depth what this rule means and what awareness and growth it offers us. The dictionary defines the word *encounter* (in verb form) as "to clash, to come up against someone or something." *Clash* implies tension. We have all experienced tension thousands of times in our life. But have we ever felt grateful for that tension, that clash, that particular encounter? Not likely.

We usually want to avoid experiences that might turn into something tense. Few among us honestly enjoy adversarial situations. But this rule offers us a new perspective on the meaning of encounters, those which are just mildly harsh and those which actually feel mean. We can interpret all encounters, whatever their nature, as blessings. All encounters are holy, not just the ones that feel good. And within each encounter is a lesson we are seeking to learn, although our search is likely unconscious.

For a moment, reflect on a difficult experience from

childhood. Re-create the experience, including the key players. Can you see how it served as a catalyst for later experiences that came to you? Our experiences aren't arbitrary.
Their impact on us is intentional. What most of us didn't
know as children was that we didn't have to go through our
experiences afraid and alone. The same Higher Power who
is present in our lives now was present then too. We may
not have celebrated that presence. We may not have even
been conscious of that presence, but it was there.

Coming to believe that every experience we have with
another person is by intention and is *holy* makes all experiences tolerable and meaningful and not very scary after all.
It's only our perspective that makes an experience or a particular person scary. And as we have learned already, we can
change our perspective at will.

The journey each one of us is making has a destination
parallel to the journey everyone else is making. The people
we need to meet along the way need to meet us, too. Our
lessons are intertwined. We cannot learn what we need to
know without others. Doesn't this realization change the
tenor of even the most difficult of our relationships?

Even after we have come to understand that every encounter is a holy encounter meant for our benefit, we may
still not be willing to glean from each of them what we need
to know. That's why it's important to remember that we will
get another opportunity, through another encounter with a
different person, to learn each missed lesson. These lessons
come again and again until we learn them.

Each of us has at least one past experience that we can't
fathom was a blessing. I have been greatly helped by the

idea that *what I believe isn't all that important*. I just need to trust that every experience was, in fact, a blessing. It did move me along the path. It was an experience I can share with at least one other human being who might be greatly helped by my sharing it. Maybe I didn't need the particular experience for my own growth as much as the person with whom I shared it did.

It's not ours to know, *in the moment*, why everything happens. It's ours to accept that we are getting what we need and we will receive comfort from our Higher Power if we seek it. Greeting each encounter like a gift can allow us to see what is really present. Resisting an encounter or creating fear around it will distort the meaning within the experience.

Over time I came to believe that I didn't have to be afraid of any experience; that each one is meant for my good. I loved the idea that, in some way, all my experiences had been handpicked by me.

I have also come to cherish the notion that even if my spiritual beliefs seem contradictory to some people, that's okay. My quest is for peace. Whatever offers peace deserves my attention and my gratitude.

Every moment in time is fleeting and can never be repeated or clung to. However, any "missed" message will be expressed once again, perhaps within another relationship. Nothing will escape us, for long, that we need to know or experience.

Our presence is essential in the lives of everyone we encounter. It's a sacred dance we are sharing with one another. Let's enjoy the music.

Touch Points

1. Every moment is sacred.
2. Every person is holy.
3. Every conversation is intentional.
4. Every experience offers us a lesson we need.
5. Our journeys are parallel and intertwined.
6. Every word we say is heard by God.
7. Every experience is handpicked by us.
8. Every person we meet has been chosen to share our path.
9. Every person we meet has volunteered for the lesson we share.
10. We need fear no experience.
11. We need not understand the journey, but we must accept it.
12. We will be grateful for every moment of the journey in due time.
13. What we believe isn't necessarily the truth.

❧ 23
No Relationship Is Accidental

I adamantly and undeniably believe that no relationship is accidental. This means even those relationships we wish we could forget were necessary to the journey we were destined to make. This isn't always easy to accept, but if we apply a bit of hindsight, we can generally glimpse the contribution a particular relationship, even a very painful one, made to the unfolding of our life.

Looking back at my first marriage gives me many opportunities to celebrate the lessons that the relationship offered me. My husband and I were both in trouble with alcohol from the first drink we took together in 1958, and we continued that pattern of drinking throughout our courtship and our twelve-year marriage. We were guilty of infidelity, physical and emotional abuse, and incessant, hateful behavior. It's fortunate that we brought no children into the world. We were not fit to be parents. Our personal problems were far too grave to have added parenting to the mix.

There were high points in the marriage, but they were few and far between. I wasn't able to see them with any clarity until long after my husband had left. In fact, I didn't see them without bias until I had been in recovery from alcoholism for several years. Prior to that point, I remained angry and hurt; I was the perfect victim.

Fortunately, I had a great sponsor in my early years of recovery. She taught me that I had bargained for every experience I either relished or suffered through before coming to this plane of existence. I was pretty skeptical of what I judged to be her "new age" wisdom, but I let it comfort me because I had no other wisdom to hang on to. Surprisingly it did comfort me quite adequately.

I came to believe that my first husband was the perfect partner to accompany me on my journey into active alcoholism, which led me to eventually become a recovering alcoholic who authored books for others in recovery. This understanding relieved me of the awful embarrassment and anguish I had felt over having been the rejected party in our marriage. Rejection, I learned, had to happen in order for me to find my way into recovery so that I could fully feel what my spirit, my inner voice, wanted to share with others. There are no accidents.

Being able to celebrate my first marriage's value has made it possible for me to transfer that same understanding to other stressful relationships. In the process, I've been able to experience sincere gratitude for all people who have ever crossed my path. There were no accidental meetings.

I didn't appreciate many people at the time of our interactions, and I can't say that I loved experiencing every trial in every relationship. I now know, though, that every person and the lessons embodied in each relationship were part of the agenda I was born to experience.

It gives me profound relief to know that I will continue

to meet who I need to meet, and that within each relationship, whether it be fleeting or well developed, I will learn what I have come here to learn. I am also relieved to know that the reason I assume someone is in my life may not be why they are present at all. Awaiting the full explanation of their presence and trusting that *more will be revealed* at the right time, has a sweetness to it.

Many people I have met on this recovery path have lamented struggles with their parents or siblings. I have shared those struggles, and, as with my first marriage, I believe that I chose the family I needed to have. I chose my family for the growth I have experienced and have eventually come to cherish because of them. I don't even need to understand this choice, really. As with so many other relationships, hindsight can offer answers, but it can also offer relief when relief is called for.

I used to be embarrassed to share this part of my personal philosophy, but the more I age, the happier I am to have a simple perspective on my life. There is nothing simpler than believing there are no accidents when it comes to who we meet, when we meet them, and why. Understanding the full ramification of a relationship will come in time.

I have, on occasion, wished I had sought a more peaceful journey earlier in my life. But that's not how my life has unfolded, and now there's very little about my life that I would change, even if I could.

Touch Points

1. Every person we see has a purpose in our life, and to acknowledge that fact will bless us.
2. Even the angry person on our path has a lesson for us.
3. It is not just love-filled people who deserve love in return.
4. We do not need to understand why someone is in our life.
5. Trusting that everyone is purposefully present is our assignment.
6. We get the partners we need for the lessons we have "requested."
7. Never lament what looked like a failed relationship.
8. Never lament any experience; instead, let it inform you.
9. Cherish both the good and the bad of the past.
10. The past has no hold over us now; the present is where our lessons lie.
11. We will continue to meet whom we need to meet.
12. We cannot avoid the lessons we need.
13. There are no coincidences.

∞ 24
To Surrender Is to Know Peace

Surrendering doesn't have to mean *giving up* in a beaten, negative way. Surrendering can be considered a choice to give up struggling, regardless of what the struggling is about. There is simply no possibility of changing another person, unless he or she is willing to change, so why struggle?

I never observed the surrendering process in my family of origin. On the contrary, I watched my dad "dig in" whenever there was a disagreement. For that matter, he seemed to dig in even when the interaction was no more than a simple discussion. He was always right, regardless of the topic. The concept of surrendering was not even remotely available in his consciousness.

The idea of willingly surrendering to another's opinion was not available to me either until I found this spiritual path. We learn what we see around us, and I didn't see people surrendering their position until I heard my fellow addicts sharing their experiences, strengths, and hopes in AA and Al-Anon. It was only then that I was able to view surrendering as a sensible option.

We don't have to lose face in the act of surrendering. That's a common misconception though, one that is easily fueled by the media's attention to the incessant battles that are happening throughout the world. World leaders simply aren't respected if they walk away from a battle. "Win at any cost," is the common battle cry. Don't back down. Don't surrender. Don't relinquish your position, ever, if you want to be revered in this culture. The problem with this approach is that people who resist surrendering at all costs are seldom, if ever, at peace.

Being at peace is my goal. I have become willing, on most occasions, to do whatever is necessary to enjoy a more peaceful existence. I don't always immediately surrender my perspective or opinion; my stubborn ego sometimes wants to win its position and hold sway over the opponent. However, every time I do choose to back away from an argument, I am generally surprised, relieved, and enlightened by the way the encounter resolves itself. We must always remember, God cannot do for us what needs to be done if we don't get out of the way.

Why is it so hard for most of us to give in? I have become convinced that it's because we equate our worthiness with being right. Many of us were raised to think about ourselves and others this way. Someone who always felt wrong lost confidence easily. Asserting that you are right and having others share your opinion is ego-inflating.

Surrendering to another person's opinion or to the majority viewpoint doesn't mean you have to agree with it. It only means you are choosing to relinquish your ground in that particular situation. It might even be appropriate to say, "I am not in agreement, but there is nothing to be gained from challenging the group right now." Then the holder of the minority opinion can be heard and the discussion can either end there or continue until a resolution is agreed upon. That way, respect for each person is demonstrated and fence-sitters can see the payoff in surrendering rather than holding up a problem that deserves resolution.

As with so many behaviors, practice lessens resistance to surrendering. Making the choice to surrender the battle becomes a sought-after choice in time. I spent the first thirty-five years of my life being argumentative and practicing being right. I got very good at this! I didn't like the idea of being peaceful. It sounded dull. I had never even wondered what being peaceful felt like. And then I got sober.

My perspective on most things began to change when I quit drinking. It had never occurred to me that drinking had fueled my rage, my insistence on being right, my unwillingness to surrender any opinion or position I held. Giving up alcohol didn't change everything about me immediately, but spending time with people who lived more peacefully began to have an effect on me. I still wanted to be right much of the time, but I was beginning to notice that others walked away from tense situations. I also noticed that chaos had a short life when at least one of the players quit playing. What a surprise this new awareness was.

The wisdom I began to glean from the words and actions of others, coupled with the desire I was developing for a gentler life, offered me moments of absolute freedom from chaos and a glimmering of peace. Nothing about my life felt familiar anymore, yet many aspects of my life felt like a gift that I hadn't known was coming.

Surrendering becomes downright delicious with practice.

I am still, on occasion, surprised when I hear myself voice the idea of surrendering as a solution to most struggles to a friend or sponsee, but I can't convey my passion for it strongly enough. Surrendering where tension abounds has absolutely changed my life. I love the joy that comes over me when I simply shut up or walk away.

I believe that the world would be well served if we all made the decision to walk away from one tense situation every day. Our feelings, our actions, even our small thoughts are impacting the rest of the universe whether we know it or not.

Each one of us has the opportunity, even the obligation, to do our part to create a better world. What easier way to make our contribution than to say or do nothing?

Touch Points

1. Surrendering doesn't mean losing or being second best.
2. Surrendering is a choice for peace rather than tension.
3. Everyone benefits from one person's willingness to surrender.
4. The sense of peace that comes over us when we surrender is intoxicating.
5. Nobody really ever wins an argument. Feelings are always hurt.
6. Until one practices walking away from a tense situation, the rewards cannot be realized.
7. Walking away from a situation that causes you unrest gives you a fresh perspective on every other tense situation too.

8. Any new behavior can become second nature with enough practice.

9. Nothing is ever gained from "digging in" with an opinion.

10. One's entire perspective begins to change as surrendering becomes more natural.

11. This world would look very different if more of us were willing to surrender.

12. If every single human being walked away from just one argument today, the entire universe would feel the shift.

13. A tiny change by any of us exponentially changes all of us.

❧ 25
Love May Fail But Courtesy Will Prevail

There is no simple definition of love, but we all recognize what love is not. It is not rageful, scary behavior. It is not physical endangerment. It is not sexual or emotional abuse. It is not needling or excessive teasing or bullying. Love is none of these.

These behaviors are actually reflections of fear, and fear is the opposite of love. Some of these behaviors are more serious than others, but they are all fairly common expressions of the fear-based person.

I have learned from more than a dozen years of studying *A Course In Miracles* that any expression of fear is a call for healing and help. It's never easy to respond with kindness when someone has entered our space in an unloving manner, but the result of responding with hate is certain escalation of a situation that doesn't need further fuel. It's not easy to walk away from this kind of experience, but the reward for doing so is immediate.

Walking away from a negative or dangerous situation is perhaps one of the most freeing experiences a person can have. Removing ourselves physically or emotionally from a set of circumstances that is destined to get ugly is unbelievably empowering. For me, it's as though a heavy weight has been lifted from my shoulders and the ball of anxiety in my stomach has suddenly dissipated.

We don't have to stay where we are not being treated with care. In fact, we should never stay in any unsafe place. We may have never attempted to escape from an emotionally or physically hurtful situation, but practicing gives us the strength to remove ourselves more quickly the next time we are in a setting that doesn't honor us or that doesn't feel safe.

Unfortunately, we may face many emotionally charged settings on a daily basis, but most of them won't require us to physically leave. However, learning that we can shift our perception of any situation just as quickly as we choose to makes these experiences far less encumbered.

This shift in perception doesn't necessarily change the circumstances. In fact, it seldom does. The perpetrator of the abuse may still be physically present, but if our attention to him or her has shifted, our experience will change too.

My life has shown me that love, in any of its forms or expressions, is elusive. Unloving behavior, however, is not elusive. We recognize unloving behavior with no difficulty, partly because it is so common. And since love is so hard to define, we can choose in its place another response that is more easily expressed: courtesy.

Courtesy is simple kindness. It can be expressed with a smile or a nod, a tiny acknowledgment that we hear or see the other person present. It can be silent or vocal. It allows the other party to know he or she is not invisible to us.

Courtesy doesn't preclude disagreement, but it does set the parameters for how a disagreement will be handled. Courtesy doesn't lead to violence; it encourages kindness as a response. People don't have to agree or even like each other very much to act courteously.

Courtesy could change the outcome of every scrimmage. It could resolve family squabbles that have gone on for decades. Perhaps it could prevent divorce. It could even change world affairs. The power, the absolute strength of courtesy would astound us if we ever really applied it to the circumstances of our lives.

Making the decision to act courteously in every circumstance, for just one day, would convince you of the power of this simple act. No relationship would feel the same if, for just one day, your every response was courteous. Your life would be transformed in every respect in the process. Love may fail, but courtesy will prevail. Give it a chance.

Touch Points

1. Making the decision to be courteous is simple.
2. We can remake the decision as often as needed each day.
3. Simply being quiet may be one way of being courteous.
4. Agreeing to disagree is courtesy.
5. Using a soft voice makes being courteous easier.
6. Looking into the face of the person we are talking to makes being courteous an easier choice.
7. Apply the Golden Rule: Do unto others as you would have them do unto you.

8. One of the first things we were taught as children was to be courteous. As adults, we need a reminder.

9. Being courteous is an easy habit to develop.

10. Deciding to be courteous takes the guesswork out of every response.

11. Courtesy makes sense.

12. Courtesy will never come back to haunt us.

13. Courtesy will make us feel good, just as it makes the people in our life feel good.

14. Courtesy requires no planning.

15. Courtesy can change every aspect of our day.

✑ 26
In Isolation, the Spirit Dies

Isolating yourself seems like the antidote to many troubling situations. Isolation seduces us. It allows us to pretend that an uncomfortable circumstance has disappeared. We may isolate ourselves when we are afraid, when we need to make a hard decision, or when we need to face a relationship issue.

It's likely that we learned how to isolate in our family of origin. Isolation served as our safety net when we needed to escape from turmoil or confusion in the family. Perhaps we practiced isolation in our early friendships.

The natural result of isolation is that nothing changes, neither the situation nor ourselves. If we expect to experience the gifts life has promised us, we must be willing to be present to the experiences and the people who have joined our path.

Needless to say, relationships of any kind rely on interaction. Wanting all relationships to be easy and nonconfrontational is not unusual, but it's not very realistic because most people allow their egos to guide their thoughts and actions.

Typically, two or more perspectives are expressed during most discussions, and agreement, or at least acquiescence, is mandatory if the relationship is to move forward. Not all relationships move forward. Some end or are merely discarded for the present time. However, every lesson that is not learned within a relationship will come back to us once again; of this we can be certain.

Isolation is one way to temporarily avoid our lessons. In the meantime, however, our spirit dies a bit each time we isolate. The dying spirit feels no gratitude, sees no solution for the struggle that made isolation attractive, and doubts the existence of God and the purpose for the Universe. All is dark, very dark for the person whose spirit is dying.

Fortunately, our spirit can be immediately resuscitated by making one tiny decision to reenter the world around us. So many wonderful changes can occur by making the tiniest decisions.

What does it matter, you might wonder, if we choose isolation? There was a time when I said, "What I do is my business and no one else's." That's still a seductive idea, but my spiritual path has taught me that we are not separate entities peopling this universe. We are interconnected; we are one, and what one of us does affects all of us.

Our thoughts have as much of an impact as our actions. We cannot escape this reality by isolating ourselves. The ripple of our action continues.

If we can't escape having an impact on others, why try to escape at all? Our isolation doesn't protect us; it only buffers us for a while. That which needs addressing will call to us again. A bit of hindsight can convince us of this.

Isolation as a solution simply doesn't make sense. Relationships cannot heal in isolation, so while we isolate ourselves, our lessons will go unaddressed, but they will not go away. That's fortunate, actually. We can go away for a while, but we will, we *must*, return eventually to the healing path that calls to us.

Our isolation harms the *whole* as it harms each one of us. Our joining with others adds to the healing of the *whole*. Having a fearless relationship demands that we stay present to the moment. Occasionally we may need to physically remove ourselves from a situation that is dangerous to our emotional and physical well being, but we should never isolate ourselves from the lesson that is real.

Let's trust the universe. Let's trust the purpose for which we are here. Let's trust that we are being shown the way to healed lives, healed relationships, a healed world. If not us, then who can carry on the work that needs to be done? It's a tiny decision to say yes and move forward to do our work. Let's answer the call.

Touch Points

1. We will not hear the messages we need if we isolate ourselves.
2. Being alone too long is seldom beneficial.
3. Isolation and meditation are not the same thing.
4. Isolation closes the door to human care and *conscious contact*.
5. Relationships allow us to heal. Isolation prevents it.

6. Isolation will not protect us. Our lessons will wait.
7. Our isolation harms ourselves and others.
8. Being in relationship with others is why we are here.
9. Opting to isolate slows the process of healing for all of us.
10. Isolation never solves a problem; it will only complicate it.

❧ 21
Forgiveness Is the Key to Happiness

It sounds glib and simple to say that forgiveness is the key to happiness, doesn't it? In some instances, it's easy to forgive a person's behavior. The rule doesn't tell us to be forgiving in just the easy instances, though—we need to be forgiving in all instances.

Perhaps we need to consider what forgiveness actually means. Forgiveness is totally letting go of any hurt or anger that resulted from someone else's actions. *Totally*. This means hurts from our childhood, which may have been intentionally cruel and unjust, along with all the minor injustices that have happened since and continue to happen daily.

We can leave no resentment buried, no cruelty unforgiven. This isn't easy, but it sounds more difficult than it really is. It sounds difficult because we have grown accustomed to categorizing, hoarding, and grading the hurts, labeling some far more serious than others.

Some hurts might have stung more at the time they were inflicted on us, but all injuries, the physical, the mental, and the emotional, are equal in their need for our forgiveness. All hurts are history, even those that happened only a moment ago.

A *Course In Miracles* teaches us that there is no order of difficulty in miracles, or anything else for that matter. In other words, all experiences, all thoughts, all behaviors are equal in value. None is of greater impact than any other. This goes for illnesses as well as injuries to the body, mind, or emotions.

The first time I heard this spiritual philosophy, I was appalled. How could cancer and a hangnail be considered equal in their impact? Or rape and a slapped hand? Surely murder or a bumped fender couldn't be equated.

With the help of further reading and countless hours of discussion with others who knew more than I knew, I decided that I didn't have to understand how this principle worked. I only had to become willing to accept it.

Coming to believe in this principle has changed every single recollection and every daily experience in my life. It has given me a hopeful, grateful perspective on everything. It has changed how I relate to every person and every circumstance in my life. It has changed all my anticipations too. This principle can work just as effectively for you.

Just imagine for a moment the freedom you might feel if you were no longer carrying the baggage of past memories of injuries with you everywhere. Just imagine how smoothly the day would unfold if you never saw current experiences through the lenses of past, painful episodes in your life?

Letting go of the past is a skill we can develop. It is a decision, first and foremost, then it takes vigilant practice and a willingness to return to the skill development stage every time we get off track.

Getting off track is to be expected. There is no shame in having to recommit to relearning the skill. We are not in a race to the end of life. We are merely trying to do our part to heal ourselves, our relationships, and in the process, our universe. It's a doable task.

Some believe that the best definition of love is forgiveness, that the two are really one and the same. When we forgive, we give up all judgments of others; we free all people to be themselves. We hold no one hostage to our way of thinking. We simply see, accept, and even express gratitude for our experiences with every person.

Forgiveness frees us at the same time that it frees the person we forgive. We are held hostage by our resentments, and we hurt ourselves more by our unforgiveness than we hurt those we are refusing to forgive.

Until we get over our unforgiveness, we simply will not find happiness. We will feel no peace as long as we have an unforgiving heart. Holding on to even one tiny resentment will prevent the peace that could be ours.

I grew up in a family where resentment was as common as the winter cold. I was taught by example that you should hold others accountable for whatever they might have done, or *not* done, that triggered the resentment.

I don't remember ever hearing forgiveness discussed or expressed in my childhood. If a person caused you harm, you never forgot it, you never forgave it, you never got over it—you never knew peace. My parents never knew peace.

Your family experiences might not match mine, but you can probably relate to the idea of hoarding resentments. We want to be washed clean of that hoarding experience, and there is only one way to do it: through forgiveness, pure and simple.

Forgiveness is considered by some to be the bottom line, the key lesson we are here to master. Still, we deserve happiness. We came here to learn lessons, but we did not sign away our right to experience happiness. It is not a trade-off.

The next time you are in a situation that triggers resentment, be grateful. It's your opportunity to advance along the learning curve. In the process, you will be bringing the rest of us along with you.

Touch Points

1. Resentments injure us.
2. Forgiveness heals us.
3. We cannot feel resentment and forgiveness at the same time.
4. All injuries from our past must be forgiven.
5. Harboring any resentment prevents any peace.
6. Regardless of the experience, it must be forgiven if we were hurt by it.
7. Our level of peace is directly proportional to our willingness to forgive past transgressions against us.
8. Wars are caused by the accumulation of unforgiven resentments.
9. The greatest deed for humankind is forgiveness.

❧ 28

Honor Your Relationships Every Day in Tiny Ways

It doesn't take much effort to honor our relationships every day in tiny ways, and the payoff can be tremendous. How difficult is it to be attentive when loved ones are speaking to you, for instance? Honoring them in this way affirms their presence and their worth, and it also offers you the opportunity for new growth. Perhaps the other person will have an awareness or an idea your own journey longed for. Remember, our relationship partners aren't coincidental to our lives.

Making a commitment to remembering this rule will change the tenor of every experience you have. It will change the experience of your fellow travelers too.

The tiny ways we can honor others are numerous. We can listen to others intently, even when we'd rather not, and we can make eye contact. Looking someone in the eyes while talking with them seems so simplistic, but it is an often overlooked opportunity for honoring that person. How often have you continued to read the paper or watch a television show when a loved one has wanted your attention? This behavior is easily changed.

Honoring another person by remembering special dates like anniversaries and birthdays is important. Even more important is remembering those experiences a loved one might be fearfully anticipating and sharing your concern, letting him or her gain strength from your attentiveness. There is power and comfort in loving and sincere attention.

Sharing a person's anxiety by praying for him or her (either with or without his or her knowledge) has an impact too. The "pray-er" will be as affected as the "pray-ee." One of the unexpected rewards from honoring others by praying for them is that our lives are miraculously eased as well.

We honor others by showing respect, by being honest though never hurtful, and by being willing to see how another's needs might supersede our own. To honor another person means refraining from seeing them as "the adversary," regardless of whether or not the situation is tense and argumentative. Instead, we must make the choice to see all other people as teachers.

Criticism does not honor. Judgment does not honor. Dishonesty does not honor. Doing for others what we want to receive in return does honor. Putting the desires of our relationship partner ahead of our own desires does honor. Gratefully seeing each person and every experience they bring to us as our next, necessary lesson honors both the giver and the receiver.

We can honor others simply by being quiet and not trying to have the last word in a discussion. We can honor them by choosing to be peaceful rather than right. We can honor by holding a loving, peaceful thought on behalf of another person, even when that person is totally unaware of our thoughts. Our thoughts have power.

Honor is never mean. It is never condescending. It doesn't ignore. It doesn't sabotage. It doesn't punish.

Honor blesses. Honor respects. Honor lifts the spirits of both the giver and the receiver. It shifts the perspective both people have of the moment and allows solutions to reign. Arguments are resolved and love is made manifest.

Every day we can decide to be honorable in all of our interactions. We can decide to show honor by how we listen and respond, by how we think and how we pray, by how we forgive. These decisions provide the substance for changing the world close to home and contribute toward changing the larger world that claims all of us as its children.

Go into today with this single thought: I will honor all those who come into my life by my thoughts, my words, my actions, and my prayers. Watch the transformation of your life. It's guaranteed.

Touch Points

1. Be kind. It's honorable.
2. Never disparage another person.
3. Practice the Golden Rule.
4. Listen, pause, and think before responding.
5. Be willing to be honorable.
6. Pray for others.
7. Regard all people as your teachers and be grateful for them.
8. Don't criticize.
9. Honor others through smiles, prayer, and thoughts of love.
10. Honor others through forgiveness.

ॐ 29

Detach with Love

As I mentioned earlier, it was more than thirty years ago that John Powell's book, *Why Am I Afraid to Tell You Who I Am?* made such an impression on me. Even though I wasn't ready to comprehend the meaning of the experience Powell related in that book, I knew his words were giving me some information I very much needed.

Let me refresh your memory. Powell and his friend stopped to buy a newspaper from a busy street corner vendor. The vendor was exceedingly rude, just as he was every other day. As they closed the transaction, Powell's friend thanked the vendor, gave him a tip, and wished him a good day. Powell asked why he continued to be kind to a man who was always so obnoxious and his friend said, "Why should I let him decide what kind of day I am going to have?"

I had spent my whole life letting other people's behavior rule my day. I honestly didn't know I had another option. I had no boundaries between myself and others. I was enmeshed in the lives of those around me, good friends and strangers alike. When they were happy, I was happy. When they were angry, I was certain it was my fault. When they were silent, I assumed it was my job to open them up and make them feel better.

It wasn't until years later, after attending many Twelve Step meetings and counseling sessions, that I heard the word *detach*. I didn't know what it meant then, but I was eventually able to see the results of successful *detachment* in the lives of certain friends.

Detaching *with love* means not doing it grudgingly, in a mean-spirited way, or by creating guilt in the other person. Detaching with love offers both people freedom from an emotional entanglement. Only by detaching from the whims, the emotions, the attitudes, and the opinions of others are we free to acknowledge, feel, and choose our own emotions.

Applying this rule in all our relationships frees us from hidden resentments or unforgiven baggage from the past— our own or someone else's. By detaching, we can let go of the opinions and the actions of others, recognizing that they reflect the other person and never us. We can allow others to be who they want to be without the complication of our judgments. When we judge others, we compromise our ability to make the right choices for our own journey.

Simply, detachment is a way of being kind to ourselves and to others. It frees us from the entanglements that prevent clear actions. Detachment does not mean lack of care. On the contrary, detaching from the turmoil another person is experiencing is one of the kindest actions we can take, both for them and for us.

When I first heard this concept discussed at an Al-Anon meeting, it sounded cold and indifferent. It sounded like turning our back on the suffering person in our life. I was used to trying to change another person's painful experiences. I had assumed this was what a loving person did.

I eventually came to understand through the help of many caring people in Al-Anon that my overinvolvement could interfere with another's journey, a journey that needed to be under God's direction, not mine.

Detaching with love allows us the opportunity for growth that we deserve. It lets others be alone without condemning them and without creating unnecessary work for ourselves. It conveys in its own language, "You are free to be you. I am here if you want my help."

The gift of this rule is that we avoid getting into the minds of others, a place we have no business being. It is not our job to be anyone else's decision maker, judge, or Higher Power.

Each of us has roles to play in other people's lives. However, that doesn't give us license to attach ourselves to the intricacies of each other's journeys. We are sharing this path, nothing more. Gently, we intersect with, accompany, and then depart from one another's path, each of us getting what we need when we need it, without judgment.

Detaching with love will improve our personal journey of healing. Through detachment, our paths will be far more peace-filled, and our relationships will be easier, kinder, and more rewarding along the way. Practice this and you will believe it too.

Touch Points

1. We honor other people when we let them make their own choices.
2. Detachment frees us.
3. Attachment binds us and cripples our growth.
4. Each person's journey is specific. We must not interfere.
5. Detachment lets us be in charge of ourselves.
6. Detachment protects our boundaries.
7. Detachment is not indifference.
8. Detachment does not mean we can't pray for another person.
9. Prayer is the one thing we can always do.
10. Detachment is the lesson common to all of us.

☙ 30

Wherever Two Are Gathered, a Third Is Present

The idea that wherever two or three are gathered, a third is present is common to many people who follow a spiritual path. Certainly it's known to those who follow the teachings of the Bible. It's a comforting thought to me, too, even though I am not a student of the Bible.

I interpret the statement to mean that every experience that involves two people always includes God. We don't have to acknowledge God's presence, but it is there nonetheless.

I said in an earlier rule that every encounter with another person is holy. The presence of the "third party" in any twosome confirms this, in my view. However, it is still a fairly elusive idea. What can't be seen with the naked eye isn't very easy to accept.

I have concluded that deciding to feel the presence of God is all that's necessary to make God's presence real. Our perspective, which grows out of our willingness to believe in God's presence, gives it the only reality it needs to positively impact our lives.

Remembering that God is looking on during our every conversation, that God is watching our every action, and that God knows our silent minds might give us reason to pause before we say or do anything. This statement is not meant to frighten you; it's meant to remind you that God's help is everywhere. We can rely on God's presence to help us handle whatever hurdles present themselves in our relationships.

Consider for a moment all the experiences you've had in the past twenty-four hours. Were you ever acutely cognizant of God's presence? Would cognizance have changed how you perceived any experience, or how you might have responded to the people present? Most likely the answer is no to the first question and yes to the second.

Our opportunity here is to remember that God is with us in every encounter, no matter how insignificant it might seem. Mundane visits to the grocery store or to the dry cleaner's are opportunities for us to practice being aware of God's presence. Anytime another person crosses our path, we have the opportunity to remember and to express the love of God.

All life experiences are practice sessions, and none of them has more significance than any of the others. Each encounter, no matter how seemingly insignificant, is our opportunity to perceive the presence of God. Knowing that the perception is possible makes our willingness to desire that perception far easier.

Being aware of God guarantees a miraculous transformation of our life. Nothing will look or feel the same when we begin the practice of acknowledging God in all ways, at all times, and with all people.

This rule in particular is guaranteed to change every person we see. How? Our "Godly" treatment of each person will nurture in them a willingness to change in the same way that our lives have changed.

This rule isn't very difficult to follow. It relies on memory followed by belief. Deciding to *see* God everywhere makes a significant difference in how our lives unfold, and it also begins a ripple effect that knows no end. Whatever we *mindfully* send forth is multiplied—the good thoughts as well as the harmful thoughts.

We sit, each one of us, in a powerful position. How we practice this rule, how we "pass it on" by our example, has the potential for significantly changing the lives of all of the people who cross our path on a daily basis. For each life we impact, countless other lives are also impacted. Our interconnectedness promises that what happens to one of us, happens to all of us.

The importance of this fact cannot be overemphasized. We are being affected by all occurrences everywhere. We don't have to see what is happening to feel its results. We can, with the knowledge of this rule, pass on worthy rewards to all people, those we specifically connect with and those who are connected to us just by being alive.

Our chances and our choices are many. What we decide to see and what we decide to say or do will live far beyond the moment of our decision. Let's be good stewards of the time we have with others today. And let's remember to remember God.

❧

Touch Points

1. God is with us this minute.
2. God is forever among us.
3. There is no discussion that cannot be helped by remembering that God is present.
4. The decision to feel God's presence is all that's needed to feel it.
5. The power of our decisions is awesome.
6. Each time any of us remembers that God is always present, we help those individuals who are not, in that moment, remembering.
7. Throughout this day, look for God's presence.
8. God is waiting for your request for help in all matters, all conversations, all decisions.

ꙮ 31
Relationships Are Why We Are Here

Healing ourselves through our relationships is our chosen path, even though few of us are aware of ever having made that choice. We simply cannot heal the pain of our individual lives alone. In isolation, our pain escalates. In time, fear and confusion overwhelm us, and we wither.

Through our collective relationships with others, we eventually learn to see and know ourselves, even though we may resist recognizing ourselves initially. Seeing must come before healing, with forgiveness wedged between.

We commonly want to deny that what we see in another person reflects back to us. However, what we see in that person is who we are, too. This is not easily accepted because it often means owning parts of ourselves that are negative.

Let's not forget we are on a journey. With a little willingness, we will learn the practice of forgiving ourselves and others, which will lessen our feelings of separateness.

With a little more willingness and wisdom, we will be able to reflect to one another the eternal presence and the love of God. This reflection strengthens our own personal awareness of God's presence while we demonstrate it for others.

We are so much more than our individual self. We are part of the whole of humanity. We are not here to struggle alone. We are here to recognize the oneness we share and to spread the message of love and forgiveness. It is only through our relationships that we are given the opportunity for doing our chosen work.

Relationships are mandatory. Without relationships, we would not have the opportunity to gather the wisdom we have been born to gather. Our interactions with one another inform us, educate us, allow us to know our purpose here, and teach us how to accomplish that purpose.

Every relationship we have, the ones we barely notice as well as the ones that last a whole lifetime, is part of the gathering of wisdom we have signed up for. We must never forget this. No person on our path should be discounted. Every person has a reason for being present in our lives, even if it is for only one tiny conversation.

The importance of this rule is easily ignored as we mind-lessly wander through our lives. How often do you take a moment to honor the person with whom you are having a conversation? Are you even paying attention? Each moment with another person, a friend, a foe, or a stranger, is full of meaning for our life. Our attention to the meaning, the moment, and the person is our responsibility.

Our easy relationships, the ones with friends who love us just as we are, offer us lessons we generally enjoy learning. Within these relationships, we don't fight the information that is presented; we know it's coming from a loving source. The absence of tension in these relationships make them far more appealing. We'd always rather learn from someone who loves us than from someone who may have a crucial, difficult lesson to teach us.

We must not shy away from difficult lessons. It's not that they are more important—there is no order of difficulty in our experiences. But they are probably less enjoyable and more intense. They may pinch rather than tickle us. However, they must be experienced. We need all of our lessons in order for us to be all that we have been called here to be.

The lessons we offer others fall into this framework too. Whoever wanders toward us needs to be in relationship with us, either because they have something to learn that we can teach or vice versa. This is exciting. It means we don't have to waste time wondering why someone is present in our lives. We need not second-guess their motives. They are present because it is our destiny and theirs.

Relationships are the substance of our lives. Without them, we would fail to make the contribution that is ours to make. People can, of course, refuse to participate in their own healing, but eventually they have to surrender to the will of God. God's will is that we heal, each one of us, and healing happens only in relationships, never in isolation.

Rejoice over your relationships, those that seem easy as well as those that are troubling. All are necessary and none will seem too difficult if we remember that they are merely the material we need to do our work. We need not fear them. Relationships are present to serve us, not hinder us. Our struggle comes from failing to understand this. Let's give up the struggle now.

Touch Points

1. Be grateful for every relationship.
2. Growth does not occur without relationships.
3. Seemingly insignificant relationships are as important as the memorable ones.
4. Difficult relationships educate us.
5. Who you see is who you are in the moment of seeing.
6. Acknowledging that we are seeing ourselves in others is the first step toward healing.
7. Our relationships teach us everything we have come here to learn.
8. Relationships are significant because they teach us how to forgive.
9. We cannot learn about love in isolation.
10. We cannot learn about forgiveness in isolation.
11. Every relationship is connected to every other relationship. None are inviolate.
12. What you give in one relationship, you are giving to all relationships.
13. We either help or hinder our relationships each time we speak.

❧ 32
Don't Try to Change the Other Person

In relationships we often wish that the other person would change, some times in major ways, often in tiny ways. This wish is wasted; we simply cannot change other people, no matter how hard we try. They may try to change to please us, but if they have not decided themselves to actually make whatever change we are demanding, it will not be permanent.

Giving up our nearly constant attempts to change others will feel extremely freeing once we get accustomed to it. It's quite a burden to be in charge of others. It feels like our work is never done when we are intent on controlling the actions and words of others. It's exhausting work, too, since our efforts are consistently futile.

Changing our perception of other people isn't easy when we first try it. We fear that when others are allowed to think and behave the way they want to, we won't be able to hold them as hostages any longer. Certainly none of us wants to admit to taking hostages, but if we are in the habit of trying to control other people, we are in the practice of hostage-taking. We imprison both the other people and ourselves by our behavior.

Another difficulty lies in the fact that we continue to

look at everyone we want to change with the same eyes that judged them so many times before. We have to be willing to look anew at the people sharing our journey. The best way I have discovered for looking anew is to seek to see the *spirit* present in my fellow travelers. This means making the decision to see within the other person, to see who he or she really is instead of our projection. We must allow our own heart to *see* the other person's heart.

Every relationship we are in right now could be significantly changed for the better if we were to take this tiny step. There is nothing wrong with taking this step selfishly. Most of us will primarily do this for ourselves the first time, but there is another major payoff for doing it. Our willingness to see our companions without judgment will foster willingness in them to see other people differently too. What a person does on behalf of one relationship is being done on behalf of all relationships simultaneously, both the good and the bad.

It's not possible to fully explain the inner change we will experience if this suggestion is adopted and practiced faithfully. Every part of our daily activities will seem different when each person is seen with fresh eyes. The proof is in the practice.

We all recognize when we are being judged, and none of us likes it. The assignment here is very straightforward— judge not. It's our judgments that encourage us to foist control on others. Our judgments prevent us from seeing who is really there to be seen. Our judgments keep us stuck in our own past and prevent us from moving peacefully to our own future.

We cannot change any other person; we can change only ourselves. As we grow to accept this fact, we will find our lives unfolding far more joyfully. We will also feel more successful knowing that we can change ourselves!

Not only can we not change other people, we cannot change any element of the world around us. We can change how we see each of those elements, though, just as we can change how we see our companions. When our perceptions change, as they can and will with a little willingness, our lives will dramatically change too. Make the decision to give up your faulty perceptions of others, just for today. Let the experience you have convince you that this suggestion, this rule, is necessary to your journey.

Touch Points

1. Not being able to change others benefits us in many ways.
2. If we were able to change others, our work would never be done.
3. Our perceptions are changeable.
4. The decision to change a perception can be made in an instant.
5. Changing one perception makes changing a second perception far easier.
6. People have minds of their own. Perceptions live in our mind only.
7. We can change our life by changing our perceptions.

8. Seeing with our heart makes changing our perceptions easier.

9. Giving up judgment will change every experience.

10. Seeing as God sees is our assignment. Practice makes this possible.

11. We have the opportunity to change the experience of our life and the lives of others every time we change our perception and see them "rightly."

12. We can change the world by changing how we see things.

❧ 33
Do No Harm

Our last rule, do no harm, can't be emphasized enough. Other rules have hinted at a similar idea. One asked us to be gentle in all our responses, and another told us to be kind at all times, but *do no harm* carries a slightly different emphasis. This rule asks us to at least refrain from harming others when we *can't* muster up kindness or gentleness.

Doing no harm emphatically means avoiding injury of any kind. We don't endanger someone's life. We don't behave recklessly around them. We are never violent. We don't use words or actions to abuse others. If we are feeling out of control in any way, we remove ourselves from the setting as a precaution against doing any harm.

Even when we don't choose kindness as a response, we don't have to be *unkind*. Likewise, resisting gentleness doesn't mean we have no choice but to be rough or rude. The responses we make in any instance are as varied as the people making the responses.

When we do no harm consistently, it becomes a mindset. How fortunate for us and for our many relationship partners that this is so. Good choices can become as habitual as bad choices. The choice to do no harm benefits every-one with whom we come into contact. It ultimately benefits everyone our acquaintances come into contact with too. There is no finality to our actions. The pattern begun goes on and on.

Let me be more specific. There are so many tiny ways we can harm others that perhaps it's easier to understand the concept of *doing no harm* by making sure we never do the following harmful things: We must never physically strike a person or publicly reprimand a person. We must never use foul language against a person or gossip about anyone. We must never set up a person for failure. We must never create difficulties between any two people as a way of serving our-selves. We must avoid being mean or hurtful at all costs. We must never do to others what would cause pain to us.

It's pretty easy for each of us to see that we have done harm to others. A quick inventory of the past will refresh our memories about many harmful actions we took. Did we make amends? Even a look back at yesterday's interactions might reveal many instances where we responded to another person in a harmful way. Were we mean because we were afraid?

Fear triggers many kinds of harmful behaviors. Consider what was on your mind right before you acted hurtfully. Was fear on your doorstep?

If fear is the root cause of our harmful actions, how might we change our behavior? Can we avoid fear? We can try. The spiritual path that comforts me has taught me that my fears are about my feelings of separation or alienation from others.

When I am feeling alone and unloved or unworthy, I blame others and seek ways to punish them. My thoughts are not necessarily conscious, but they are as effective and powerful as if they were.

Harming someone else, in even the tiniest way, serves as a quick remedy for our own unhappiness, or so we think. Thank goodness it doesn't work. However, we are seldom aware of how miserably this remedy has failed until after we have hurt others by it. At that point, we feel unworthy and we have caused others to feel sad or unworthy too. Their hurt feelings do not alleviate our own.

The way out of all of this turmoil is to simply decide that we will never do anything to another person that we would not want done to us. This is a simple, straightforward decision that leaves no room for confusion. It allows for no waffling. Even if someone does an unkind thing to us, we do not have the right to react in kind.

To do no harm means to never, under any circumstance, act in a way that causes injury, great or small, recognized or unrealized, to another person. If this becomes our guiding principle for living, if this were the only "rule" and we applied it diligently to our lives every day, we would greatly enhance the quality of every relationship we have. If even a few people were truly committed to doing no harm, the world would never be the same. What an idea!

Touch Points

1. Our actions and words are either harmless or they are not.
2. We can decide to do no harm without having to actually be kind if kindness feels too difficult.
3. Doing no harm can become, with very little practice, an easy choice.
4. Doing no harm may mean remaining quiet or walking away from the situation.
5. Doing no harm can mean doing nothing at all.
6. Doing no harm is a shortcut to improved relationships.
7. Doing no harm in one relationship will improve all relationships.
8. Any harm we do anywhere affects every person alive, everywhere.
9. Doing no harm is the least complicated choice to make in any relationship.

❧ Closing Thoughts

It's by design that you and I have come to know each other through the pages of this book. It's by design that each of us has come to know everyone who has been on our path throughout the journey. This idea gives me great comfort. It assures me that I will always be in the right place at the right time. I will meet individuals who need to know me just as much as I need to know them. Of course, this is true for you as well.

Those of us who have come to rely on this idea to sustain us are lucky people. It will continue to sustain us for as long as we honor this information by being willing to let it guide us and give us peace.

Peace is what I long for, and I assume it's what you long for too. It's what I have found each time I have let one of the suggestions in this book be my focus for a day or even for just a moment. Any one of these rules, even marginally applied, has the power to change my life. I am confident that they can change your life too. We don't have to do them all. Picking one for the day is quite enough.

As was pointed out in this book many times, our willingness to change in a positive way, even one small detail of our life, will foster a change in the lives of everyone we come into contact with. This is how the world changes: one tiny positive act at a time.

We can do our part for peace each time we open our mouths, each time we convey an opinion by our body language, each time we harbor a thought. Let's be ready. Let's acknowledge how empowered we really are. Let's add to the peace of all humanity, one small step at a time.

May peace be with you, now and always.

❧ About the Author

Karen Casey is the best-selling author of *Each Day a New Beginning*, *Daily Meditations for Practicing the Course*, *Keepers of the Wisdom*, and numerous other books. She has also written two books for girls: *Girls Only!* and *Girl to Girl*. Her signature book, *Each Day a New Beginning*, has sold three million copies. Karen enjoys golfing and riding her Harley with her husband. She lives in Minneapolis, Minnesota, and Naples, Florida.

Hazelden Publishing and Educational Services is a division of the Hazelden Foundation, a not-for-profit organization. Since 1949, Hazelden has been a leader in promoting the dignity and treatment of people afflicted with the disease of chemical dependency.

The mission of the foundation is to improve the quality of life for individuals, families, and communities by providing a national continuum of information, education, and recovery services that are widely accessible; to advance the field through research and training; and to improve our quality and effectiveness through continuous improvement and innovation.

Stemming from that, the mission of this division is to provide quality information and support to people wherever they may be in their personal journey—from education and early intervention, through treatment and recovery, to personal and spiritual growth.

Although our treatment programs do not necessarily use everything Hazelden publishes, our bibliotherapeutic materials support our mission and the Twelve Step philosophy upon which it is based. We encourage your comments and feedback.

The headquarters of the Hazelden Foundation are in Center City, Minnesota. Additional treatment facilities are located in Chicago, Illinois; New York, New York; Plymouth, Minnesota; St. Paul, Minnesota; and West Palm Beach, Florida. At these sites, we provide a continuum of care for men and women of all ages. Our Plymouth facility is designed specifically for youth and families.

For more information on Hazelden, please call **1-800-257-7800.** Or you may access our World Wide Web site on the Internet at **www.hazelden.org.**